"*A Miracle Awaits* fills an important niche among titles introducing the Catholic faith. Its brief summaries of essential Catholic teachings are highly accessible, and the hands-on components provide both concrete instruction and motivation for growth in the practice of the Sacraments, the moral life, and Catholic prayer. Notable assets include the carefully selected lists of recommended readings and websites. This excellent little handbook on Catholicism will be an invaluable tool for participants in RCIA, as well as new and returning Catholics."

Elizabeth Siegel
Co-author of *A Year with the Catechism: 365 Day Reading Plan*

"Are you looking for a quick overview of Catholic faith and practice for yourself or someone you know who is interested in learning more? This concise, practical book is a good place to start!"

Heidi Saxton
Author, editor, and blogger at "Life on the Road Less Traveled"

A MIRACLE AWAITS
ENCOUNTERING CHRIST IN HIS CHURCH

A CATHOLIC GUIDEBOOK

CAROL DINTELMAN

Nihil Obstat: Monsignor Terence Nolan, JCL
Vicar for Canonical Affairs of Archdiocese of San Antonio, TX
March 19, 2019

Copyright © 2019 Carol Dintelman. All rights reserved.

Published by Garland of Roses Media
GarlandOfRosesMedia.com

ISBN: 978-1-7339464-0-7
eISBN: 978-1-7339464-1-4

Unless otherwise noted, Scripture texts in this work are taken from the New American Bible, revised edition © 2010, 1991, 1986, 1970 Confraternity of Christian Doctrine, Washington, D.C. and are used by permission of the copyright owner. All rights reserved. No part of the New American Bible may be reproduced in any form without permission in writing from the copyright owner.

Excerpts from the English translation of the *Catechism of the Catholic Church* for use in the United States of America, Second Edition, copyright © 1997, by the United States Catholic Conference—Libreria Editrice Vaticana. Used with permission.

Every reasonable effort has been made to secure permissions and give proper credit to excerpted materials in this book. If any copyrighted materials have been used without proper credit given, please notify GarlandOfRosesMedia.com so the issue can be corrected.

Cover and interior design by Carol Dintelman

No part of this publication may be reproduced, stored in a retrieval system, or transmitted in any form or by any means—electronic, mechanical, photocopy, recording, or any other—except for brief quotations in printed reviews, without the prior permission of the author and publisher.

Made and printed in the United States of America

Photos:

Cover: Pilgrimage Church of the Assumption of Mary, Lake Bled, Slovenia ©Shchipkova Elena - stock.adobe.com.

Pages 16 - 17: The Church of St. Michael the Archangel, Dražovce, Slovakia ©kaycco - stock.adobe.com.

Introduction: Mother, father, and daughter looking at sunset ©nazariykarkhut - stock.adobe.com.

1. Encountering God: Cathedral of the Immaculate Conception, Chanthaburi, Thailand ©Thissatan - stock.adobe.com.

2. Encountering Christ: Sacred Heart Statue ©Richard Kane - stock.adobe.com.

3. Catholic Church - Truth: Statue of St. Peter at St. Peter's Basilica, Rome, Italy ©ggaallaa - stock.adobe.com

4. Sacraments: Church of St. John the Baptist, Bohinjsko jezero, Slovenia ©zkbld - stock.adobe.com

5. The Mass: The Minor Basilica and Metropolitan Cathedral of the Immaculate Conception, also known as Manila Cathedral, Manila, Philippines ©Wayne S. Grazio - stock.adobe.com.

6. Mary, Saints, Angels: Statue of Mary and Baby Jesus ©Karel Miragaya - stock.adobe.com.

7. Challenging Topics: Batalha Monastery, Batalha, Portugal ©StockPhotosArt.com - stock.adobe.com.

8. Life Issues: The Original Tilma at the Basilica of Our Lady of Guadalupe, Mexico City, Mexico ©NoraDoa - stock.adobe.com. (Our Lady of Guadalupe is the Patroness of the Unborn.)

9. What Must I Do? Basilica of Saint Francis of Assisi, Assisi, Italy ©immagine e file protetti dai Diritti D'Immagine - stock.adobe.com.

10. Living the Faith: Statue of St. Paul at St. Peter's Basilica, Rome, Italy ©magogiuppy - stock.adobe.com

11. Practices: St. Joseph's Catholic Church, San Antonio, Texas ©Garland of Roses Media - garlandofrosesmedia.com.

12. Prayers: Temple of the Sacred Heart of Jesus, Mount Tibidabo, Barcelona, Spain ©itsmejust - stock.adobe.com.

13. Calendar: Notre-Dame Basilica, Montreal, Quebec, Canada ©jiawangkun - stock.adobe.com.

14. Growing in Faith: Notre Dame de la Garde chapel, Etretat, Normandy, France ©stevanzz - stock.adobe.com.

To my daughter Nicole Grace

TABLE OF CONTENTS

INTRODUCTION
19 My Faith Journey
23 How to Use This Book
24 Before You Begin

1. ENCOUNTERING GOD
27 Who Is God?
28 God's Relationship with Us: Why Did He Create Us?
28 Salvation through Jesus Christ
29 Getting Right with God (Justification)
30 About Grace

2. ENCOUNTERING CHRIST
33 Kerygma: Jesus' Message
34 Get To Know Jesus in the Gospels
35 Converse with Jesus in Prayer
37 Meet Jesus in the Sacraments

3. THE CATHOLIC CHURCH REVEALS TRUTH
41 The Pillar and Foundation of Truth
42 Scripture, Tradition, and the Magisterium
44 Christian Timeline
48 The Pope, a Closer Look
49 The Catholic Church's Key Players

4. SACRAMENTS: GOD'S GIFTS TO US

53 What Are the Sacraments?
54 Baptism: Becoming a Child of God
56 Reconciliation: Confessing Our Sins
58 The Eucharist: The Real Presence Is Real!
60 Confirmation: Come, Holy Spirit
62 Marriage: The Two Become One
64 Holy Orders: A Special Calling
67 Anointing of the Sick: Not Just for the Dying

5. THE MASS: THE SOURCE OF LIFE

71 The Culmination of Our Faith
72 The Mass Is Biblical
74 The Mass: The Word of God, the Sacrifice, and the Eucharist
77 Mass Responses

6. MARY, SAINTS, AND ANGELS

83 The Virgin Mary: Mother of God, and Our Mother
84 The Communion of Saints
85 Angels

7. SOME CHALLENGING TOPICS

89 Suffering
91 Chastity
92 The Four Last Things: Death, Judgment, Heaven, and Hell
94 Purgatory
95 Spiritual Warfare Is Real
96 Miracles

8. LIFE ISSUES

99 Life Is a Gift
100 Openness to Life
101 Embracing Life from Conception to Natural Death
103 A Child Is a Gift, Not a Right

9. WHAT MUST I DO?

107 Obey God's Law
109 Grow in Virtue
111 Be Open to the Holy Spirit

10. LIVING THE FULLNESS OF THE CATHOLIC FAITH

115 Pray
116 Prepare
119 Participate
119 Practice
120 Persevere
121 A Lively Catholic's To-Do List

11. CATHOLIC PRACTICES: HOW AND WHY

125 Eucharistic Adoration
126 Genuflection
127 Sacramentals
127 The Sign of the Cross
128 Holy Water
128 The Rosary
129 Fasting and Abstinence
130 Relics

12. CATHOLIC PRAYERS

135 Essential Prayers
140 The Divine Praises
141 Novenas
141 Litanies
142 The Rosary
148 The Chaplet of Divine Mercy

13. CATHOLIC CALENDAR

151 Advent
152 Christmas
154 Lent
154 Easter
156 Ordinary Time
156 Holy Days of Obligation
157 Solemnities, Feasts, and Memorials
158 Monthly Devotions

14. GROWING IN THE CATHOLIC FAITH

161 Building a Catholic Faith Foundation
163 EWTN, The Eternal Word Television Network
164 Documentaries
164 Catholic News
164 Other Resources

167 Notes

Acknowledgements

I am very grateful to Lucy Scholand, whose expertise helped immensely in the development of this book. A special thanks is due to Elizabeth Siegel for theological review and additional editing. Heather Turner offered her careful eye for proofreading, which I appreciate greatly. I also express my deepest gratitude to my husband, Juan, whose encouragement and support throughout this project has been a great blessing. And most of all, I thank God for his endless love and mercy.

What no eye has seen, nor ear heard, nor the heart of man conceived, what God has prepared for those who love him.

(1 Corinthians 2:9, RSV)

INTRODUCTION

*And I will give to you a new heart,
and I will place in you a new spirit.*

Ezekiel 36:26

MY FAITH JOURNEY

I'm Catholic! That's been true all my life. But being excited about the Catholic faith is a more recent development.

I was raised Catholic with loving parents, my mom a Catholic and my dad a Baptist. We went to Mass together every Sunday, I received the sacraments, and my mom was very involved in our parish. Despite all this, God didn't seem to have a big role in our lives. We didn't discuss him very much, and the occasional grace said on holidays was the extent of our prayer.

Growing up, I had a few encounters with God but nothing

that my anxious spirit absorbed. Activities, friends, and high school drama characterized my teen years, and I struggled with some anxiety that I tried to ignore. I stopped going to Mass at the end of high school. My life revolved around having a good time—partying and going out whenever I wanted while anxiously seeking love, acceptance, and praise.

After college, I entered a period of searching that led me to Costa Rica. There I met my husband. We lived in Costa Rica for several years, then moved back to the United States, where I pursued influence, business prowess, and financial stability. From the outside, I probably looked like a decent person, but my lifestyle was selfish and I was indifferent about important issues. Religion and spirituality seemed like a hobby for those who needed it. I thought God supported whatever level of participation one felt comfortable with, that we are all free to do what we want and create our own truth, as long as it makes us happy and doesn't hurt anyone.

In my mid-thirties, God used certain trials to draw me out of this toxic version of myself and closer to him. A parasite that I had picked up in Costa Rica gave me one of the worst years of my life, as I suffered difficult and embarrassing physical symptoms and, along with them, increasing anxiety. Then my husband and I tried to conceive a child, a two-year process that ended tragically in miscarriage. Now starting to grasp the fragility of life, I was joyfully relieved when I conceived my daughter. But fear for this pregnancy's outcome, along with serious medical complications, hit me to the core.

Through these experiences, I was pried away from my party lifestyle. I felt completely stripped, grasping for meaning amid sufferings over which I had no control. I found myself turning to God, even though I didn't really know how. C.S. Lewis perceptively noted this phenomenon in his book *The Problem of Pain*:

We can ignore even pleasure. But pain insists upon being attended to. God whispers to us in our pleasures, speaks in our conscience, but shouts in our pains: it is His megaphone to rouse a deaf world.[1]

Following these ordeals were some profound moments in which God touched my heart. My beloved grandfather died, and the Baptist minister at the funeral said, "The only thing Robert wanted in life was for everyone he knew to know and love Jesus as he did." I felt a pain in my heart. Not only was I missing my lovable, quick-witted, Marine Corps granddad, but I was not living up to his deep desire. The Holy Spirit was working in me. This was my first experience with the communion of saints, as I believe that my granddad's prayers aided me in my discovery of faith.

Now more open to God, I attended a Christian moms' group, where I heard the testimony of a woman who had experienced drugs, alcohol, and abortion before encountering Christ. Tears filled my eyes, and I knew I wanted to grow closer to God and find a church to attend. My husband and I had been sporadically going to Mass, but I was open to looking at other Christian churches. My mother-in-law kept pushing us to get our daughter baptized Catholic. I gave in and read up on Catholic baptism, which led me to a class on YouTube covering the fundamentals of the Catholic faith.[2] What I encountered blew me away.

I learned that Jesus Christ started a church through which all his teachings would be preserved and shared to the end of time, that this is the Catholic Church. I discovered the *Catechism of the Catholic Church*, a book that explains Catholic belief in detail. I learned about the office of the pope, the authority of sacred tradition, Scripture, and the magisterium, where the Bible came from, and more. The Catholic Faith was what the first Christians believed and practiced, coming straight from Jesus Christ. I was sold.

The event that finally launched me into aligning my life to God's will came one seemingly ordinary day when I fell extremely ill. That night, propped up in bed with fever and severe body aches, nursing my baby as my husband slept next to me oblivious, all the bad choices of my past came crashing down on me. An intense suffering, both physical and mental, set me in a spiral of despair and self-pity. Then a thought cut through and interrupted my suffering, *a thought that was not my own*: "Put God first." In that instant, I understood and agreed.

The next morning, I was completely well. I had a paradigm shift. What I had researched about the Catholic faith went from my mind to my heart and soul. I couldn't just learn about the Catholic faith; I had to live it by putting God first, at the center of my life. I immediately prepared for my daughter's baptism and my marriage convalidation in the Catholic Church. I wanted nothing more than to follow everything God was asking of me.

Our household went into spiritual crisis as I confronted my reluctant husband on contraception and other issues. I also sensed a dark presence in our home. Eventually some things in our lives that were not of God came to light, including New Age practices such as Law of Attraction. Once we removed those, the dark presence left.

My husband had his own personal experience of God's love, and our daughter was baptized. For the first time in thirty years, I received God's forgiveness and grace in the sacrament of reconciliation. Then our marriage was made right with God through the convalidation ceremony. I was immersed in pure peace and joy. This was God's love. When I received the Eucharist the first several times, I experienced Jesus' physical embrace in my soul.

I started to notice God speaking to me—through songs, radio programs, books, and Scripture. Natural creation took on a supernatural beauty. How had I failed to notice the wonder of simple things like clouds, rainbows, and wildlife?

I am very thankful for the absolutely unmerited gift of faith. I hold no regrets about the past or anxieties about the future and know that my life has meaning. I see God's love flowing in our family, which gives me the greatest joy.

HOW TO USE THIS BOOK

When I realized how little I knew about the Catholic faith, it really shocked me. I wanted to create a resource that would help others understand Catholicism, embrace it, and start living with Christ as their focus. My goal was to present straightforward explanations of core Catholic beliefs and accurate Christian history, along with ways I have found helpful in growing closer to Christ. I hope you find this book a resource to further your own faith journey and to share with family and friends.

This book is set up like a guidebook, with headings and graphics to help you navigate to the content you need. Of course, reading cover to cover works great too. You might not know what you don't know! Reading recommendations at the end of each chapter will help you study topics in more depth. I suggest you pick up two resources right away:

- a good Catholic Bible, such as the *Revised Standard Version,* Catholic Edition (Ignatius Press) or the *New American Bible,* Revised Edition.

- Catechism of the Catholic Church, Second Edition. I indicate quotes from the *Catechism* by *CCC,* followed by the paragraph number.

BEFORE YOU BEGIN

Encountering God is exciting and probably easier than you think. God is with you right now. He loves you as if you were the only person who ever existed. Keep that in mind as you go through this book and get introduced or reintroduced to God.

I suggest you pray before you begin reading:

God, I want to know you in a personal way. Please help me approach you in humility and gratitude, as your child. Open my heart to faith, and help me understand your truth. AMEN.

SUGGESTED READING

- *Atheist to Catholic: Stories of Conversion*, Rebecca Vitz Cherico.

- *Night's Bright Darkness: A Modern Conversion Story*, Sally Read.

- *Not God's Type: An Atheist Academic Lays Down Her Arms*, Holly Ordway.

- *The Problem of Pain*, C.S. Lewis.

- *The Seven Storey Mountain*, Thomas Merton.

- *Something other than God: How I Passionately Sought Happiness and Accidentally Found It*, Jennifer Fulwiler.

1
ENCOUNTERING GOD

Whoever is without love does not know God,
for God is love.
1 John 4:8

WHO IS GOD?

God the Holy Trinity is the central mystery of Christianity. There is one God, always and forever, who consists of three distinct persons:

God the Father (a pure spirit and the almighty Creator).

God the Son (who became man—Jesus Christ).

God the Holy Spirit (the Counselor or Spirit of Truth, who dwells in every baptized person).

God created the entire universe, everything you can see and everything you cannot see. God knows everything and is everywhere all at once. He transcends time. He is perfect love and perfect goodness.

GOD'S RELATIONSHIP WITH US: WHY DID HE CREATE US?

Of all the living things God created, only man and woman are created in his likeness. As the *Baltimore Catechism* (an early American Catholic catechism) states: "God made me to **know** him, to **love** him, and to **serve** him in this world, and to be happy with him forever in the next."[3] We come to **know** God through prayer, Scripture reading, and reception of the sacraments. We **love** God through worship, obedience, and loving the people around us. We **serve** God by using the gifts he has given us to glorify him and bring others to him.

Walking with God in these ways will lead us to his kingdom and eternal salvation. This is God's will for us. "Man . . . is called to share, by knowledge and love, in God's own life. It was for this end that he was created, and this is the fundamental reason for his dignity" (*CCC*, 356).

SALVATION THROUGH JESUS CHRIST

The first humans, Adam and Eve, separated themselves from God by a devastating and disobedient action referred to as original sin (see Genesis 3). The results: humans have a nature inclined to sin and experience physical death. Yet God promised to send a redeemer. Jesus, the Second Person of the Holy Trinity, came to open heaven to us. Through Jesus, all of humanity has the gift of salvation and can live forever with God in his kingdom.

In Jesus, God did the unthinkable: he humbled himself to become a man, born a helpless infant dependent on the care of other humans, so that he could save us from our sins. Out of love for each one of us, Jesus became the ultimate sacrifice. He took the weight of all of our sins on himself, dying a humiliating and excruciatingly painful death, and then rising victorious over all evil. He did it all so that you and I can live eternally with God.

Jesus is the path on this earthly pilgrimage to our true home, life forever in union with God. Jesus Christ is "the way and the truth and the life" (John 14:6).

GETTING RIGHT WITH GOD (JUSTIFICATION)

God is fair, generous, and loving, and he offers us eternal life through Jesus Christ. But we need to cooperate with God in the purification of our souls. By faith we accept Jesus Christ as our redeemer. The Holy Spirit then calls and equips us to follow God and serve him. Our obedience to God, our cooperation with his grace, is crucial to our salvation and that of the world.

We cannot merit being right with God. "This vocation to eternal life . . . depends entirely on God's gratuitous initiative, for he alone can reveal and give himself" (*CCC*, 1998). Our good works are responses to God's grace, not reasons for it. In chapter 10, "Living the Fullness of the Catholic Faith," we'll talk about how to receive and cooperate with God's grace.

ABOUT GRACE

Grace is a gift from God, a tool that helps us on our faith journey. "Grace is favor, the free and undeserved help that God gives us to respond to his call to become children of God, adoptive sons, partakers of the divine nature and of eternal life" (*CCC*, 1996; see John 1:12-18, 17:3; Romans 8:14-17; 2 Peter 1:3-4). This grace can be manifested in physical ways, or God might simply give us the strength to be humbler or more loving. In whatever way we receive his grace, we know it is from God because it increases the virtues of faith, hope, and love in us, brings peace, and encourages us to do his will.

It is exciting to see grace making us better people. Jesus Christ works in us, by the power of the Holy Spirit. We should always welcome God's grace and thank him for it.

SUGGESTED READING

- *Answering Atheism, How to Make the Case for God with Logic and Charity*, Trent Horn.

- *The Case for a Creator: A Journalist Investigates Scientific Evidence that Points toward God*, Lee Strobel.

- *The Gift of Faith*, Fr. Tadeusz Dajczer.

- *Grace & Justification: An Evangelicals Guide to Catholic Beliefs*, Stephen Wood.

- *Made for Love, Loved by God*, Fr. Peter John Cameron, OP.

- *New Proofs for the Existence of God: Contributions of Contemporary Physics and Philosophy*, Fr. Robert J. Spitzer, SJ.

2

ENCOUNTERING CHRIST

*I am the good shepherd, and I know
mine and mine know me.*

John 10:14

KERYGMA: JESUS' MESSAGE

Jesus is the most important figure in the history of mankind, and he has a powerful message for us. It is an invitation that we can word like this:

> **I am God, and I have come to you because I love you. I have come to redeem you, by sacrificing myself to save you from sin and the corruption that is in the world, so that you can participate in the divine nature, which is the very life of God. Trust in me. Turn away from other pursuits, and follow me. Do not be afraid.** (See John

10:30, John 15:9, John 3:16-17, 2 Peter 1:4, Mark 10:21, Matthew 16:24, John 14:1, Matthew 14:27)

This proclamation is called the kerygma, from the Greek words meaning "proclaim" and "herald." This kerygma is an instrument of divine power: the person who hears it and responds as Jesus intends will enter into the mystery of God's love, knowing him personally and being transformed by that love. The kerygma is the heart of the Gospel. Understanding it is the first step in encountering Jesus. And so we look to the Gospels in order to know Jesus.

GET TO KNOW JESUS IN THE GOSPELS

The Gospels are the divinely inspired documentation of Jesus' actual words and actions while he walked the earth. There are four Gospels, the first four books of the New Testament: Matthew, Mark, Luke, and John. These books are the heart of the whole Bible because they relay the powerful teachings of our Redeemer.

The formation of these writings came in three stages. First was the actual life and teaching of Jesus, then came the oral transmission of these events by the apostles, and finally this tradition was written down by the sacred authors under the inspiration of the Holy Spirit (see *CCC*, 126). Each Gospel writer presents the events and teachings of Christ in a different way, illuminating different details.

The intentionally revealed events of Jesus' life and teachings in the Gospels share something very important: Christ's life is a manifestation of God the Father's love for us (see *CCC*, 516). Jesus Christ, the Son of God, the long-awaited Messiah, teacher, healer, and Savior, is honest, loving, and challenging—calling us to give up everything and follow him.

There are several ways to approach reading the Gospels; the easiest and most obvious is to simply start reading. The Gospel of Mark is the shortest and probably the oldest, so many people start there. I suggest you purchase a Catholic Bible, pray for guidance, and dive in. There are several Catholic guides and commentaries to assist you, such as *The Catholic Commentary on Sacred Scripture* series (Baker Publishing) and the *Six Weeks with the Bible* series (Loyola Press). To find a Catholic Bible study group in your area, check your church bulletin or go to Ascension Press's website, ascensionpress.com/study/map_search.

A Gospel reading is part of daily Mass, so reading that each day is good also. The daily readings are posted on several websites and on different apps, such as the Catholic Daily Readings app (Daily Apps Co.) or the Laudate app. Reflections on the daily Gospel are posted on Evangeli.net (M&M Euroeditors, S.L.). Keeping a journal of specific ways the Gospel inspires you can encourage you and help you grow closer to Jesus.

CONVERSE WITH JESUS IN PRAYER

We know from reading the Gospels that prayer is important to God. We see that Jesus prayed to the Father often, day and night (see Matthew 14:23; Luke 11:1). His pattern of prayer is the model for how our prayer life should be. Prayer connects us closely with God and teaches us to lean on him for everything. Prayer is part of God's perfect plan for our existence. It makes a difference not just in our lives but also in the lives of others.

"Christian prayer is cooperation with his [God's] providence, his plan of love for men" (*CCC*, 2738). If we pray, we will encounter Jesus Christ. "In prayer the Holy Spirit unites us to the person of the only Son, in his glorified humanity" (*CCC*, 2673).

In theory, prayer should be very easy. It is essentially talking to Jesus, telling him everything, just as we would a spouse, close friend, sibling, or parent. So why does something so easy become so difficult to continue regularly? We might think at times that there is no point to prayer, that we are not being heard, or that it feels dry, with no consolation. These are common difficulties, part of the spiritual battle Christians face. The key to prayer is to push through these thoughts and just do it and do it often, no matter how we feel.

If prayer seems difficult, these tips might help:

Schedule It: Scheduling prayer into our day might be the only way to make sure we actually pray. We make appointments for everything, so why not put Jesus on the calendar? Our time with him is the most beneficial time of the day. Once we start praying at set times, prayer will naturally become part of our lives.

Create a Prayer Space: A peaceful and comfortable place for prayer is a wonderful addition to any home. A crucifix, an image of Jesus, candles, and other objects can help us focus on our divine guest.

Pray Out Loud: Sometimes our thoughts dart from one thing to another. If we talk aloud, as we would to any other person, we might find it is easier to focus.

Sit in Silence: We can sit in silence and look at a crucifix or a picture of Jesus—just be in his presence and listen.

Show Love and Gratitude: We might fall into the habit of continuously asking God for things. We must remember to tell Jesus that we love him and to thank him for everything he has done for us—for our lives and for all our blessings. There is so much to be grateful to Jesus for.

Pray in Everyday Situations: We can cultivate the habit of including Jesus in everyday occurrences. For example, we can thank him quietly during a joyful moment and ask him for courage during a difficult one.

Pray with Family and Friends: Jesus tells us that when two or three are gathered, he is there (see Matthew 18:20). God wants us to pray with each other and for each other.

Don't Hold Back: It's okay to express anger, confusion, and other emotions in prayer. Jesus already knows our thoughts and feelings, good and bad, and talking them out with him is exactly what he wants us to do. This is a very healing practice.

Meditate on Scripture and Other Spiritual Reading: Praying in this manner acquaints us with God and his ways, deepening our relationship with him.

MEET JESUS IN THE SACRAMENTS

The sacraments connect us with Jesus and pour into our souls his love and grace. "The sacraments are perceptible signs (words and actions) accessible to our human nature. By the action of Christ and the power of the Holy Spirit they make present efficaciously the grace that they signify" (*CCC*, 1084).

Jesus desired to create tangible ways he could be present to us after he ascended into heaven, so he instituted the seven sacraments: baptism, confirmation, Eucharist, reconciliation, marriage, holy orders, and anointing of the sick. These are dispensed through his Church, the Catholic Church, by ordained bishops, priests, and deacons. When we receive the sacraments, we share in the divine life of God. He is made present within us, to transform and guide us to eternal life.

The sacraments are very generous gifts from God. His intention is that we utilize them frequently. God literally pours out his love for us through the sacraments, giving us life in Christ. "Sacraments are 'powers that come forth' from the Body of Christ, which is ever-living and life-giving. They are actions of the Holy Spirit at work in his Body, the Church. They are 'the masterworks of God' in the new and everlasting covenant" (*CCC*, 1116).

Please refer to chapter 4 for information on each sacrament.

SUGGESTED READING

- *The Bible Compass: A Catholic's Guide to Navigating the Scriptures*, Edward Sri.

- *The Gospel of Mark (Catholic Commentary on Sacred Scripture)*, Mary Healy.

- *Jesus of Nazareth*, three volumes, Pope Benedict XVI.

- *Jesus: What Catholics Believe*, Alan Schreck.

- *The Life of Christ*, Abp. Fulton Sheen.

- *Time for God*, Fr. Jacques Philippe.

- *To Know Christ Jesus*, Frank J. Sheed.

3

THE CATHOLIC CHURCH REVEALS TRUTH

The household of God . . . is the church of the living God, the pillar and foundation of truth.
1 Timothy 3:15

THE PILLAR AND FOUNDATION OF TRUTH

The Catholic Church presents God's truth—not just one set of opinions about theology and morality, but the teachings of Christ as revealed in Scripture and passed down through the apostles and their successors. When we embrace the Catholic Church, we allow ourselves to be immersed in truth and align our lives accordingly.

This is not to say that everything every Catholic says and does is true. Every individual—woman and man, even the pope—is human and thus sinful and will make mistakes, even grave ones. But we can count on the Catholic Church to teach the truth.

It is important to understand our faith. We must be sure that the information we receive is true to Catholic teachings. We can do this by referring to the Bible, the *Catechism of the Catholic Church*, and other resources that the Catholic Church approves. A *nihil obstat* and *imprimatur* on the copyright page of a book indicates that the work agrees with Catholic teaching.

SCRIPTURE, TRADITION, AND THE MAGISTERIUM

Where do Catholic teachings come from? When Jesus was on earth, he taught about God's infinite love and his kingdom. He taught us how to access the gift of eternal life, life in union with God forever. In order to pass this good news on to all of humanity, Jesus chose twelve men to be his apostles. These "were to communicate the gifts of God to all men" (*CCC*, 75).

The entirety of what Jesus taught the apostles is called the *deposit of faith*. Jesus made the Catholic, or universal, Church the protector and guardian of the deposit of faith for all time. He promised that "the gates of the netherworld shall not prevail against it" (Matthew 16:18) and that he would guide the Church "until the end of the age" (Matthew 28:20).

From the time Jesus started the Catholic Church two thousand years ago, her beliefs have stayed the same. They are true to the deposit of faith given to the apostles by Jesus Christ.

Catholic bishops are direct successors of the original apostles, and the pope is the successor of the lead apostle, Peter. "In order that the full and living Gospel might always be preserved in the Church the apostles left bishops as their successors. They gave them their own position of teaching authority" (*CCC*, 77).

One of the first things the apostles did after Jesus ascended into heaven was to fill the empty office left by Judas Iscariot; they selected Matthias (see Acts 1:13-26). Later we see "presbyters" appointed in different churches (see Acts 14:23). The letters to Timothy and Titus give guidelines on the selection of bishops (see 1 Timothy 3:1-7; Titus 1:5-9). Thus the succession from the original apostles began, and it continues with the Catholic bishops of today.

The Catholic Church professes that "Sacred Scripture is the speech of God as it is put down in writing under the breath of the Holy Spirit" (*CCC*, 81). Jesus' ascension into heaven occurred around the year AD 33. The canon of Scripture, consisting of the books deemed truly inspired by the Holy Spirit, was established over 300 years later, at the end of the fourth century. The bishops at the Synod of Hippo discerned what writings should belong in the canon of Scripture. The criteria included that the writings of the New Testament must be of apostolic origin and conform to the oral traditions of the Catholic Church. The canon consists of forty-six Old Testament books and twenty-seven New Testament books (see *CCC*, 120).

Jesus promised to protect the teaching of his Church by the guidance of the Holy Spirit, who would guarantee the correct interpretation of sacred Scripture and the accurate transmission of the faith. The Holy Spirit acts through the teaching office of the Church, which is referred to as the *magisterium*. The magisterium "is not superior to the Word of God, but is its servant. It teaches only what has been handed on to it. At the divine command and with the help of the Holy Spirit, it listens to this [the Word of God] devotedly, guards it with dedication, and expounds it faithfully" (*CCC*, 86).

Whoever listens to you listens to me. Whoever rejects you rejects me. And whoever rejects me rejects the one who sent me. (Luke 10:16)

Christian Timeline

AD 30 - 33

Jesus starts the Catholic Church, appoints Peter as head over the Church, and promises that the Church will endure.

[Jesus] said to them, "But who do you say that I am?" Simon Peter said in reply, "You are the Messiah, the Son of the living God." Jesus said to him in reply, "Blessed are you, Simon son of Jonah. For flesh and blood has not revealed this to you, but my heavenly Father. And so I say to you, you are Peter, and upon this rock I will build my church, and the gates of the netherworld shall not prevail against it. I will give you the keys to the kingdom of heaven. Whatever you bind on earth shall be bound in heaven; and whatever you loose on earth shall be loosed in heaven." (Matthew 16:15–20)

Jesus revealed God and his plan of salvation to the apostles through words and actions. He gives them divine authority to pass on this faith to all nations.

Then Jesus approached and said to them, "All power in heaven and on earth has been given to me. Go, therefore, and make disciples of all nations, baptizing them in the name of the Father, and of the Son, and of the holy Spirit, teaching them to observe all that I have commanded you. And behold, I am with you always, until the end of the age." (Matthew 28:18 – 20)

John the Evangelist makes the point that **Jesus showed more** to the apostles than can be contained in writings.

There are also many other things that Jesus did, but if these were to be described individually, I do not think the whole world would contain the books that would be written. (John 21:25)

50 - 96

New Testament books are written. The Church grows amid persecution.

110

First surviving documented use of the term **"Catholic Church"** (universal church), to refer to the church Jesus started, in the writings of Ignatius of Antioch, a Catholic bishop known as one of the Early Church Fathers.[4] Persecution of Christians continues.

306
Constantine becomes emperor, and will bring an end to Christian persecution.

325
The Nicene Creed formally defines the fundamental beliefs of the Catholic Church.

382 and following
St. Jerome translates the Greek and Hebrew texts of Scripture into Latin, the language of the Roman Empire.

386
Augustine is converted to Christianity and becomes bishop of Hippo. His writings will help shape Western Christianity and philosophy.

393
At the Synod of Hippo, Catholic bishops discern which documents will be accepted into the canon of Scripture (**the Bible**). The criteria include that the writings of the New Testament must be of apostolic origin and conform to the oral traditions of the Catholic Church.

480
St. Benedict writes his rule to guide monasteries in a life of prayer and service to God.

621
Muhammad introduces **Islam**, which will challenge Christianity for centuries.

1054
Issues in the **Eastern churches** lead to their separation from the Catholic Church.

CATHOLIC CHURCH - TRUTH

1200s

St. Francis of Assisi and St. Dominic inspire many to greater faith and devotion through their preaching and teaching.

1492

Columbus discovers America, opening a new mission field for the Church.

1517

Martin Luther breaks from the Catholic Church. Protestant denominations will eventually number in the thousands. Jesus intended unity, not separation of Christians. He wanted everyone to follow exactly what he taught the apostles. As St. Paul wrote in the first century:

I urge you, brothers, in the name of our Lord Jesus Christ, that all of you agree in what you say, and that there be no divisions among you, but that you be united in the same mind and in the same purpose. (1 Corinthians 1:10)

1531

The Blessed Virgin Mary's appearance in Tepeyac, under the name Santa María de Guadalupe, sparked the conversion of some ten million people to the Church over the next decade.

1534

King Henry VIII breaks from the Catholic Church to form the **Anglican Church** or Church of England.

1545

Council of Trent. The bishops meet to defend and clearly restate Catholic doctrines that are under attack through the Protestant Reformation. The council also addresses numerous abuses in the Church. It is important to note that no Catholic teachings were changed at the Council of Trent.

The No. 1 priority was to defend clearly Catholic beliefs...the belief that Christ instituted seven sacraments, not two as asserted by Luther; that justification was achieved by faith and good works, not by faith alone; that the deposit of faith included both the sacred Scriptures and sacred Tradition, not the Scriptures alone; that Communion of one kind for laypeople is sufficient to receive the Real Presence; that the traditional teachings on transubstantiation and original sin are correct; that purgatory does exist; that Masses for the dead are appropriate. These were affirmations, not changes, to Catholic beliefs. In a like manner, the conciliar decrees that defended the Mass were based on unchanging truths and revelation, not on innovation.[5]

1640's

St. Isaac Jogues and others spread the faith in America, with many losing their lives for the faith.

1789

The Archdiocese of Baltimore is the **first diocese** established in the United States.

1917

The Blessed Virgin Mary appears to three children in Fátima, Portugal, to warn of coming troubles and the need for prayer.

1962-1965

The Second Vatican Council meets to invigorate the Church for her mission in the world.

1968

Pope Paul VI issues "Humanae Vitae" ("Of Human Life"), confirming the Church's teaching on the transmission of human life.

1984

Pope John Paul II initiates **World Youth Day**, to bring young Catholics together for prayer, instruction, and community.

2000

Jubilee Year commemorates the **two-thousandth anniversary of the Son of God becoming man**.

2015

Pope Francis announces the **Holy Year of Mercy**.

THE POPE, A CLOSER LOOK

The head of the Catholic Church is Jesus Christ, and the Catholic Church is his body:

> And [the Father] put all things beneath [Jesus'] feet and gave him as head over all things to the church, which is his body, the fullness of the one who fills all things in every way. (Ephesians 1:22-23)

The pope (also called the Holy Father, the bishop of Rome, and the vicar of Christ) is the earthly leader of the Catholic Church. He is a direct successor of the lead apostle, Peter. The Bible tells us that Jesus Christ appointed Peter as chief of the apostles. Jesus changed Peter's name from Simon to Peter, meaning "rock," and said, "Upon this rock I will build my church" (Matthew 16:18). *The Catholic Encyclopedia*, at newadvent.org, gives the complete line of popes from St. Peter to Pope Francis.[6]

Many people think that the Catholic Church teaches that the pope is correct in everything he says and that he cannot sin. This is a misconception of the Church's teaching on infallibility. The pope speaks infallibly only when 1) he is speaking on a subject of faith or morals, 2) is speaking as the Vicar of Christ to the whole Church, and 3) specifies that he is speaking *ex cathedra*, that is, from the official seat or office of St. Peter (see *CCC*, 891). The pope is subject to sin and goes to confession like every other Catholic.

Many of the popes are great saints who have contributed to our understanding of the Christian faith and accomplished much for the glory of God. St. John Paul II is considered one of the greatest saints of modern times. He made World Youth Day a notable phenomenon, affirmed the "feminine genius," promulgated the *Catechism of the Catholic Church*, canonized 482 saints, and earned the title "Pope of the Family" through his wonderful teachings on love and marriage, known as the Theology of the Body.

THE CATHOLIC CHURCH'S KEY PLAYERS

The Pope

The earthly leader of the Catholic Church and successor of the lead apostle, Peter.

Cardinals

High officials in the Catholic Church and counselors of the pope.

Bishops

Chief ministers who possess the fullness of the priesthood, their office is in direct succession to that of the apostles, they preside over a diocese, and submit to the primacy of the pope.

Priests

Ministers, coworkers of bishops, taking on supporting roles and sharing in the bishops' consecration and mission.

Deacons

Ministers of charity, administer certain sacraments, preach, and support the bishops and priests.

Religious Orders

Priests, Monks, Friars:
Men who commit themselves to a particular religious community with specific vocations and charisms.

Nuns and Sisters:
Women who commit themselves to a particular religious community with specific vocations and charisms.

Laity

Members of the Christian faithful who are not ordained clergy or religious.

If you remain in my word, you will truly be my disciples, and you will know the truth, and the truth will set you free.

John 8:31-32

SUGGESTED READING

- *Catholic Christianity: A Complete Catechism of Catholic Beliefs Based on the Catechism of the Catholic Church*, Peter Kreeft.

- *The Compact History of the Catholic Church*, Alan Schreck.

- *Crossing the Threshold of Hope*, Pope John Paul II.

- *Crossing the Tiber: Evangelical Protestants Discover the Historical Church*, Stephen K. Ray.

- *Four Witnesses: The Early Church in Her Own Words*, Rod Bennett.

- *Surprised by Truth: 11 Converts Give the Biblical and Historical Reasons for Becoming Catholic*, Patrick Madrid.

- *Where We Got the Bible: Our Debt to the Catholic Church*, Henry Graham.

- *Why Catholic Bibles Are Bigger: The Untold Story of the Lost Books of the Protestant Bible*, Gary G. Michuta.

- *Why I Am Catholic (and You Should Be Too)*, Brandon Vogt.

- *Yours Is the Church: How Catholicism Shapes Our World*, Mike Aquilina.

4

SACRAMENTS: GOD'S GIFTS TO US

So let us confidently approach the throne of grace to receive mercy and to find grace for timely help.
Hebrews 4:16

WHAT ARE THE SACRAMENTS?

Jesus Christ instituted the sacraments of the Catholic Church. God knows that humans are physical beings, so he created ways for us to make contact with him through these outward signs that convey his grace. There are seven sacraments. Baptism, confirmation, and the Eucharist are the sacraments of Christian initiation, which bring us into the fullness of Christian life. Reconciliation and the anointing of the sick are the healing sacraments. Holy orders and matrimony are the sacraments of ministry. The sacraments are usually received in the following order: baptism, reconciliation,

Eucharist, confirmation, holy matrimony or holy orders, and anointing of the sick.

BAPTISM: BECOMING A CHILD OF GOD

The sacrament of baptism is the door to becoming children of God and members of the Body of Christ. The Church bestows baptism at the earliest possible point in life, in infancy or after conversion to Christ and instruction in the faith. Baptism cleanses us of sin, makes us adopted children of God, and incorporates us into the Church, the family of God (see *CCC*, 1213).

The visible sign of baptism is water, signifying cleansing and rebirth. The water is poured over the head, or the person is immersed in the water, with the words, "I baptize you in the name of the Father, and of the Son, and of the Holy Spirit." Baptism seals the Christian with an indelible spiritual mark, which not even sin can erase from the soul. "Given once for all, Baptism cannot be repeated" (*CCC*, 1272).

Bishops, priests, and deacons are the ordinary ministers of baptism. But anyone, even an unbaptized person, can baptize in cases of necessity. This is because the Church recognizes baptism as necessary for salvation. Jesus said, "No one can enter the kingdom of God without being born of water and Spirit" (John 3:5). At the same time, the Church entrusts the unbaptized to God's mercy. *"God has bound salvation to the sacrament of Baptism, but he himself is not bound by his sacraments"* (*CCC*, 1257, emphasis original).

When an ordained person baptizes, he also anoints the person with sacred oil. This signifies the gift of the Holy Spirit.

We can look at infant baptism this way: if a child was dying of a serious illness, we would certainly take him to the doctor for treatment. We would not wait until the child was old enough to understand the illness or make a decision for himself on treatment; this would be absurd. Baptism is a spiritual treatment for our souls, uniting us to God's family, which is the most important relationship of our lives.

Baptism in Scripture

 I will sprinkle clean water over you to make you clean; from all your impurities and from all your idols I will cleanse you. I will give you a new heart, and a new spirit I will put within you. I will remove the heart of stone from your flesh and give you a heart of flesh. I will put my spirit within you so that you walk in my statutes, observe my ordinances, and keep them. (Ezekiel 36:25-27)

Jesus answered, "Amen, amen, I say to you, no one can enter the kingdom of God without being born of water and Spirit." (John 3:5)

Whoever believes and is baptized will be saved; whoever does not believe will be condemned. (Mark 16:16)

Peter [said] to them, "Repent and be baptized, every one of you, in the name of Jesus Christ for the forgiveness of your sins; and you will receive the gift of the holy Spirit. For the promise is made to you and to your children and to all those far off, whomever the Lord our God will call." (Acts 2:38-39)

Now, why delay? Get up and have yourself baptized and your sins washed away, calling upon his name. (Acts 22:16)

God patiently waited in the days of Noah during the building of the ark, in which a few persons, eight in all, were saved through water. This prefigured baptism, which saves you now. It is not a removal of dirt from the body but an appeal to God for a clear conscience, through the resurrection of Jesus Christ. (1 Peter 3:20-21)

Let us approach with a sincere heart and in absolute trust,

with our hearts sprinkled clean from an evil conscience and our bodies washed in pure water. (Hebrews 10:22)

RECONCILIATION: CONFESSING OUR SINS

Confession is a powerful and healing sacrament for soul, mind, and body. It is a necessary step in the process of sanctifying our souls. For "all have sinned and are deprived of the glory of God" (Romans 3:23).

Why do we go to a priest to be forgiven of sins? Jesus gave authority to his apostles to forgive sins on his behalf. "'Receive the holy Spirit. Whose sins you forgive are forgiven them, and whose sins you retain are retained'" (John 20:22-23).

The priest is not the one forgiving us. Rather, Jesus works through the priest to bestow grace and mercifully cleanse us from our sins. The only condition for receiving forgiveness is a sincere desire to amend our lives and to try our best not to fall into those sins again. Frequent visits to the confessional, even for minor sins, are beneficial in growing closer to God.

Remember that God created this sacrament for us and wants us to use it. "Therefore, confess your sins to one another and pray for one another, that you may be healed" (James 5:16). Check your local church bulletins or website, or look under the "confessions" tab on **masstimes.org**, to see when and where confession is offered in your area.

After telling the priest your sins, he will ask you to say an Act of Contrition (see chapter 12, "Catholic Prayers"; often a copy is available in the confessional). Then the priest will give you a penance, usually some prayers or a specific act of mercy, and absolve you in the name of the Father, and of the Son, and of the Holy Spirit. He will say, "Go in peace"; a suitable response is "Thank you, Father."

Five Aspects of a Good Confession

1. Examine your conscience. (Chapter 10, "Living the Fullness of the Catholic Faith," includes an examination of conscience based on the Ten Commandments.) A nightly examination of conscience (reviewing the day and pinpointing moments of despair, weakness, and temptation) is helpful.

2. Be truly sorry for your sins.

3. Tell your sins to the priest. Include all sins of which you are aware and their frequency.

4. Resolve not to commit these sins again.

5. Do the penance the priest gives you.

The Sacrament of Reconciliation in Scripture

Amen, I say to you, whatever you bind on earth shall be bound in heaven, and whatever you loose on earth shall be loosed in heaven. (Matthew 18:18)

[Jesus] said to them again, "Peace be with you. As the Father has sent me, so I send you." And when he had said this, he breathed on them and said to them, "Receive the holy Spirit. Whose sins you forgive are forgiven them, and whose sins you retain are retained." (John 20:21-23)

So whoever is in Christ is a new creation: the old things have passed away; behold, new things have come. And all this is from God, who has reconciled us to himself through Christ and given us the ministry of reconciliation, namely, God was reconciling the world to himself in Christ, not counting their trespasses against them and entrusting to us the message of reconciliation. So we are ambassadors for Christ, as if God were appealing through us. We implore you on behalf of Christ, be reconciled to God. (2 Corinthians 5:17-20)

Therefore, confess your sins to one another and pray for one another, that you may be healed. The fervent prayer of a righteous person is very powerful. (James 5:16)

THE EUCHARIST: THE REAL PRESENCE IS REAL!

Catholics believe that Jesus Christ is fully present—body, blood, soul, and divinity—in every particle of the consecrated bread and every drop of wine of Holy Communion. This is *the* greatest gift God gives us in the Church. Through the Holy Eucharist, God heals and sanctifies our souls. As we give ourselves to God at Mass, he gives us his only Son.

Jesus instituted the Holy Eucharist at the Last Supper, and he told the apostles, "Do this in memory of me" (Luke 22:19). Thus Jesus gave his priests the power to consecrate the bread and wine into his Body and Blood. This power is passed on to other men through priestly ordination. (See the section "Holy Orders: A Special Calling" in this chapter.)

At the consecration during Mass, the physical aspects of the bread and wine (taste, smell, and so on) remain, while the *substance* of the bread and wine (what they actually are) is changed to the Body and Blood of Jesus Christ. Every particle of the bread and every drop of the wine are forever changed into the glorified and risen Christ. This is referred to as transubstantiation.

The consecrated hosts that remain after Mass are kept in a tabernacle in the church. A red candle burns near the tabernacle, to remind us of Jesus' presence. We genuflect reverently whenever we enter the presence of the Blessed Sacrament.

Many churches offer adoration of the Blessed Sacrament, in which the host is displayed in a windowed receptacle called a monstrance.

If you struggle to believe in the real presence of Jesus Christ in the Eucharist, ask God for help. Start by praying, "Lord, I do believe, help my unbelief" (Mark 9:24).

The Eucharist in Scripture

Then he took the bread, said the blessing, broke it, and gave it to them, saying, "This is my body, which will be given for you; do this in memory of me." And likewise the cup after they had eaten, saying, "This cup is the new covenant in my blood, which will be shed for you. (Luke 22:19-20)

But they urged him, "Stay with us, for it is nearly evening and the day is almost over." So he went in to stay with them. And it happened that, while he was with them at table, he took bread, said the blessing, broke it, and gave it to them. With that their eyes were opened and they recognized him, but he vanished from their sight. (Luke 24:29-31)

Jesus said to them, "I am the bread of life; whoever comes to me will never hunger, and whoever believes in me will never thirst. (John 6:35)

I am the living bread that came down from heaven; whoever eats this bread will live forever; and the bread that I will give is my flesh for the life of the world." (John 6:51)

Jesus said to them, "Amen, amen, I say to you, unless you eat the flesh of the Son of Man and drink his blood, you do not have life within you. Whoever eats my flesh and drinks my blood has eternal life, and I will raise him on the last day. For my flesh is true food, and my blood is true drink. Whoever eats my flesh and drinks my blood remains in me and I in him. Just as the living Father sent me and I have life because of the Father, so also the one who feeds on me will have life because of me. (John 6:53-57)

The cup of blessing that we bless, is it not a participation in the blood of Christ? The bread that we break, is it not a participation in the body of Christ? Because the loaf of bread is one, we, though many, are one body, for we all partake of the one loaf. (1 Corinthians 10:16-17)

CONFIRMATION: COME, HOLY SPIRIT

Confirmation is an essential sacrament that completes the grace of baptism in us. As with baptism, we receive confirmation only one time in our lives, as our souls are sealed forever with the Holy Spirit. Through confirmation, we are given "a special strength of the Holy Spirit" (*CCC*, 1303), as were the apostles at Pentecost, to fearlessly spread the message of Jesus Christ by word and action. Confirmation also roots us more deeply in our role as children of God, unites us more closely to Christ, increases the gifts of the Holy Spirit within us, and makes our bond with the Church more perfect (see *CCC*, 1303).

In the Latin Rite, confirmation is administered at "the age of discretion" (*CCC*, 1307). The American bishops administer the sacrament to children between seven and sixteen years of age.

The bishop usually administers this sacrament to people of his diocese, which demonstrates that the sacrament's effect is to unite the recipient "to the Church, to her apostolic origins, and to her mission of bearing witness to Christ" (*CCC*, 1313). The bishop may delegate this faculty to a priest. The minister anoints the candidate's forehead and lays his hands on the candidate while praying, "Be sealed with the gift of the Holy Spirit."

Confirmation is vital for Christian formation. The candidate must carefully prepare by studying the faith in order to fully profess it, and by receiving the sacrament of reconciliation. The recipient is taking on the role of an intentional disciple of Jesus Christ.

What if you are confirmed but have never known what the sacrament means? God always meets us where we are. His Spirit is at work in you, perhaps bringing you to this point of understanding. If your lack of appreciation of the sacrament lays heavily on your conscience, you can address it the next time you go to confession. Know that through God's merciful love, we are forgiven for our past shortcomings.

Let us thank God for the extraordinary gift of this sacrament, through which we receive even more grace from the Holy Spirit to aid us in our vocation.

Confirmation in Scripture

> Now when the apostles in Jerusalem heard that Samaria had accepted the word of God, they sent them Peter and John, who went down and prayed for them, that they might receive the holy Spirit, for it had not yet fallen upon any of them; they had only been baptized in the name of the Lord Jesus. Then they laid hands on them and they received the holy Spirit. (Acts 8:14-17)

> When they heard this, they were baptized in the name of the Lord Jesus. And when Paul laid [his] hands on them, the holy Spirit came upon them, and they spoke in tongues and prophesied. (Acts 19:5-6)

> But the one who gives us security with you in Christ and who anointed us is God; he has also put his seal upon us and given the Spirit in our hearts as a first installment. (2 Corinthians 1:21-22)

MARRIAGE: THE TWO BECOME ONE

God created man and woman as complements to one another. The two become one flesh when they enter into the sacrament of holy matrimony.

> So they are no longer two, but one flesh. Therefore, what God has joined together, no human being must separate. (Matthew 19:6)

Christ instituted this sacrament as an indissoluble union. The couple enters a sacred covenant with one another, just like God's covenant with man and Christ's covenant with his Church. The giving of the entire self to the other is ordered toward the procreation of children, the blessed fruits of this union.

Marriage creates rights and duties between the man and woman and toward their children. Spouses are responsible for the holiness of one another, and as parents they are expected to educate their children in the Catholic faith. Remember that sacraments are founts of grace. Through holy matrimony, God infuses us with grace to live out this covenant in conformity with his will. "[T]he spouses receive the Holy Spirit as the communion of love of Christ and the Church. The Holy Spirit is the seal of their covenant, the ever-available source of their love and the strength to renew their fidelity" (*CCC*, 1624; see Ephesians 5:32).

This grace results in love flowing within the marriage and family, which reflects God's love for us and is a tangible sign of Christ's presence:

> "[Christ] encounters Christian spouses through the sacrament of Matrimony." Christ dwells with them, gives them the strength to take up their crosses and so follow him, to

rise again after they have fallen, to forgive one another, to bear one another's burdens, to "be subject to one another out of reverence to Christ," and to love one another with supernatural, tender, and fruitful love. In the joys of their love and family life he gives them here on earth a foretaste of the wedding feast of the Lamb:

"How can I ever express the happiness of a marriage joined by the Church, strengthened by an offering, sealed by a blessing, announced by angels, and ratified by the Father? . . . How wonderful the bond between two believers, now one in hope, one in desire, one in discipline, one in the same service! They are both children of one Father and servants of the same Master, undivided in spirit and flesh, truly two in one flesh. Where the flesh is one, one also is the spirit." (*CCC,* 1642)

Given the indissoluble nature of a valid and sacramental marital union, the Catholic Church does not recognize divorce as a way to dissolve this union. In certain cases, however, civil divorce might be necessary for legal reasons. There are marriages that would be considered invalid for various reasons, and a decree of nullity can be sought in such circumstances.

Marriage is between one man and one woman. Partnerships of other types—same-sex, multiple parties, and so on—cannot be considered marriages. Loving, loyal, and *chaste* friendships among people of the same or opposite sex are, however, an integral part of life. Please see more about chastity in chapter 7.

Holy Matrimony in Scripture

He said in reply, "Have you not read that from the beginning the Creator 'made them male and female' and said,

'For this reason a man shall leave his father and mother and be joined to his wife, and the two shall become one flesh'? So they are no longer two, but one flesh. Therefore, what God has joined together, no human being must separate." (Matthew 19:4-6)

"For this reason a man shall leave [his] father and [his] mother and be joined to his wife, and the two shall become one flesh." This is a great mystery, but I speak in reference to Christ and the church. In any case, each one of you should love his wife as himself, and the wife should respect her husband. (Ephesians 5:31-33)

For the husband is head of his wife just as Christ is head of the church, he himself the savior of the body. As the church is subordinate to Christ, so wives should be subordinate to their husbands in everything. Husbands, love your wives, even as Christ loved the church and handed himself over for her to sanctify her, cleansing her by the bath of water with the word, that he might present to himself the church in splendor, without spot or wrinkle or any such thing, that she might be holy and without blemish. So [also] husbands should love their wives as their own bodies. He who loves his wife loves himself. For no one hates his own flesh but rather nourishes and cherishes it, even as Christ does the church, because we are members of his body. (Ephesians 5:23-30)

HOLY ORDERS: A SPECIAL CALLING

Christ entrusted to his apostles the mission of going out and making disciples of all peoples. Through the sacrament of holy orders, this mission continues in his Church.

Jesus is the one and only High Priest, yet his priesthood is made present in the three degrees of holy orders: episcopate (bishops), presbyterate (priests), and diaconate (deacons). In the service of the men who receive the sacrament of holy orders, "it is Christ himself who is present to his Church as Head of his Body, Shepherd of his flock, high priest of the redemptive sacrifice, Teacher of Truth" (*CCC*, 1548).

Bishops hold the chief position among the ministers, as their office is in direct succession to that of the apostles. Priests are coworkers of bishops, taking on supporting roles and sharing in the bishops' consecration and mission. Deacons can minister the sacraments of baptism and holy matrimony. They preach, teach, administer, and support the bishops and priests. Transitional deacons are preparing for the priesthood; permanent deacons are, well, permanently deacons.

The sacrament of holy orders is administered by a bishop with the laying on of hands and prayer, following the example of the apostles in sacred Scripture. Through this action, God's grace is given to the ministers being ordained.

The presence of Christ in a minister does not preserve him from human weakness, error, and sin, but the power of the Holy Spirit through the sacraments administered by the minister is still guaranteed (see *CCC*, 1550).

Only baptized men are candidates for the sacrament of holy orders. Jesus specifically selected men to be his apostles, and they in turn selected men as their successors. The Church is bound by this decision of Jesus Christ, making the ordination of women impossible. This in no way takes away from the invaluable place of women in the Church and in salvation history. God created the Blessed Virgin Mary as a perfect creature, spared her from original sin, and chose her to give birth to and raise Our Lord. Women are held in high regard within the Church, as St. John Paul II proclaims in his writings. (See his encyclical "On the Dignity and Vocation of Women" ["Mulieris Dignitatem"] and his "Letter to Women", both posted on the Vatican website, Vatican.va.)

The sacrament of holy orders is crucial to the life of the

Church, as it is through ordained ministers that we receive the other sacraments and their accompanying graces. Ordained ministers are Christ's instruments.

Holy Orders in Scripture

Then Jesus approached and said to them, "All power in heaven and on earth has been given to me. Go, therefore, and make disciples of all nations, baptizing them in the name of the Father, and of the Son, and of the holy Spirit, teaching them to observe all that I have commanded you. And behold, I am with you always, until the end of the age." (Matthew 28:18-20)

So the Twelve called together the community of the disciples and said, "It is not right for us to neglect the word of God to serve at table. Brothers, select from among you seven reputable men, filled with the Spirit and wisdom, whom we shall appoint to this task, whereas we shall devote ourselves to prayer and to the ministry of the word." The proposal was acceptable to the whole community, so they chose Stephen, a man filled with faith and the holy Spirit, also Philip, Prochorus, Nicanor, Timon, Parmenas, and Nicholas of Antioch, a convert to Judaism. They presented these men to the apostles who prayed and laid hands on them. (Acts 6:2-6)

While they were worshiping the Lord and fasting, the holy Spirit said, "Set apart for me Barnabas and Saul for the work to which I have called them." Then, completing their fasting and prayer, they laid hands on them and sent them off. (Acts 13:2-3)

For this reason, I remind you to stir into flame the gift of God that you have through the imposition of my hands. For God did not give us a spirit of cowardice but rather of power and love and self-control. So do not be ashamed of your testimony to our Lord, nor of me, a prisoner for his sake; but bear your share of hardship for the gospel with the strength that comes from God. (2 Timothy 1:6-8)

ANOINTING OF THE SICK: NOT JUST FOR THE DYING

Jesus Christ is our divine physician. He instituted the sacrament of anointing of the sick in order to heal us, body and soul. God often uses illness as a way to convert our hearts and show us how to lean on him. With his merciful love and forgiveness, God is the ultimate healer. He teaches us that our suffering through illness can have meaning and redemptive value.

The graces received through the sacrament of anointing of the sick include strength, peace, and courage to overcome the difficulties of both body and soul. God forgives sins through this sacrament. He often restores health. He also offers through this sacrament preparation for passing into eternal life. The Holy Spirit renews hope and faith in us, that we may reject temptation and unite ourselves more closely to Christ. Our suffering can yield redemption for ourselves and others.

Anointing of the sick is not just for the dying. Anyone with a serious illness (physical or mental), an upcoming surgery, or weakening caused by old age can receive this sacrament. God wants to give grace to renew us and heal us according to his will.

Anointing of the Sick in Scripture

> They drove out many demons, and they anointed with oil many who were sick and cured them. (Mark 6:13)

> Is anyone among you sick? He should summon the presbyters of the church, and they should pray over him and anoint [him] with oil in the name of the Lord, and the prayer of faith will save the sick person, and the Lord will raise him up. If he has committed any sins, he will be forgiven. (James 5:14-15)

God is able to make every grace abundant for you, so that in all things, always having all you need, you may have an abundance for every good work.

2 Corinthians 9:8

SUGGESTED READING

- *7 Secrets of Confession*, Vinny Flynn.

- *Catechism of the Catholic Church*, part 2, "The Celebration of the Christian Mystery."

- *The Catholic Church Saved My Marriage: Discovering Hidden Grace in the Sacrament of Matrimony*, Dr. David Anders.

- *From Darkness to Light: How One Became a Christian in the Early Church*, Anne Field, OSB.

- *Marriage: The Rock on Which the Family Is Built*, William E. May.

- "Familiaris Consortio" ["The Role of the Christian Family in the Modern World"], Pope John Paul II. (This encyclical is available at the Vatican website, vatican.va)

- *Sober Intoxication of the Spirit: Filled with the Fullness of God* and *Sober Intoxication Part Two: Born Again of Water and the Spirit*, Fr. Raniero Cantalamessa, OFM Cap.

5
The Mass: The Source of Life

*The bread that I will give is my flesh
for the life of the world.*

John 6:51

THE CULMINATION OF OUR FAITH

The Mass is literally heaven on earth. This is where the miracle of our faith culminates and where we absorb the Word of God, participate in the greatest sacrifice to God, and receive Jesus Christ in the Eucharist. At Mass our souls are sanctified and nourished by the Bread of Life, Jesus himself. The Second Vatican Council stated that the Mass is the "source and summit of the Christian life" (*CCC*, 1324). It is important that we recognize it as such and take part in it with attention and reverence.

THE MASS IS BIBLICAL

In his audio CD, "The Mass Explained," Fr. Larry Richards explores the Bible passages that prepare for the revelation of the Mass.[7] He explains how God has been preparing man for the Mass from the time of his first covenant with Abraham. When Abraham, our father in faith, went up the mountain to sacrifice Isaac in obedience to God, he said, "My son, ... God himself will provide the sheep for the burnt offering." (Genesis 22:8). Later, John the Baptist recognized Jesus as that offering: "He saw Jesus coming toward him and said, 'Behold, the Lamb of God, who takes away the sin of the world'" (John 1:29).

At the Last Supper, Jesus gave us the sacrifice of the Eucharist for all time:

> When the hour came, he took his place at table with the apostles. He said to them, "I have eagerly desired to eat this Passover with you before I suffer, for, I tell you, I shall not eat it [again] until there is fulfillment in the kingdom of God." Then he took a cup, gave thanks, and said, "Take this and share it among yourselves; for I tell you [that] from this time on I shall not drink of the fruit of the vine until the kingdom of God comes." Then he took the bread, said the blessing, broke it, and gave it to them, saying, "This is my body, which will be given for you; do this in memory of me." And likewise the cup after they had eaten, saying, "This cup is the new covenant in my blood, which will be shed for you." (Luke 22:14-20)

Jesus tells us that he eagerly desires to share his body, blood, soul and divinity with us. He tells the apostles to "do this in memory" of him (Luke 22:19). This is a loving command, not a suggestion.

After Jesus' resurrection, he meets two of his disciples on the road to Emmaus. At first they do not recognize him. What follows is a Mass. Jesus cites Scripture and interprets it for them (the readings and homily, or Liturgy of the Word). When they reach their destination, they say, "Stay with us." Jesus stays with them, as he stays with all of us through the Bread of Life, the sacrament of the Holy Eucharist. Upon consuming Jesus' body, blood, soul, and divinity, the disciples recognize Jesus (see Luke 24:27-35). We too must open our eyes and see Jesus' presence in the Eucharist.

The Eucharist is the Body and Blood of Jesus. Jesus made this apparent in what is called the Bread of Life discourse:

> "I am the bread of life. Your ancestors ate the manna in the desert, but they died; this is the bread that comes down from heaven so that one may eat it and not die. I am the living bread that came down from heaven; whoever eats this bread will live forever; and the bread that I will give is my flesh for the life of the world."
>
> The Jews quarreled among themselves, saying, "How can this man give us [his] flesh to eat?" Jesus said to them, "Amen, amen, I say to you, unless you eat the flesh of the Son of Man and drink his blood, you do not have life within you. Whoever eats my flesh and drinks my blood has eternal life, and I will raise him on the last day. For my flesh is true food, and my blood is true drink. Whoever eats my flesh and drinks my blood remains in me and I in him. Just as the living Father sent me and I have life because of the Father, so also the one who feeds on me will have life because of me. This is the bread that came down from heaven. Unlike your ancestors who ate and still died, whoever eats this bread will live forever." (John 6:48-58)

Jesus made his point so clear that many of his disciples left because they couldn't believe it. Jesus did not back down; he wanted people to understand this teaching. "The words I have spoken to you are spirit and life" (John 6:63).

Jesus Christ is present in every particle of the consecrated bread and every drop of wine. While the "accidents" (taste and appearance) remain, the substance is truly changed to Jesus Christ. We refer to this miracle as transubstantiation. It occurs at every Mass.

THE MASS: THE WORD OF GOD, THE SACRIFICE, AND THE EUCHARIST

The Mass is composed of the Liturgy of the Word and the Liturgy of the Eucharist. In the Liturgy of the Word, readings are proclaimed from the Bible, the inspired Word of God. On Sundays and some feast days, we hear four passages from sacred Scripture: one from the Old Testament, the Acts of the Apostles, or Revelation; a Psalm response, often sung; one from a New Testament letter; and one from a Gospel. At weekday Masses, there are usually just three readings: one from the Old Testament or a New Testament letter, a Psalm response, and a Gospel reading. The priest will then give a homily, a message based on the readings or on the day's feast.

Why do we call the Mass the "holy sacrifice of the Mass"? What is the sacrificial aspect? This is the principal element of the Mass. The Mass is the same sacrifice as that of Jesus on the cross: "The Eucharist is . . . a sacrifice because it *re-presents* (makes present) the sacrifice of the cross, because it is its *memorial* and because it *applies* its fruit" (*CCC*, 1366, emphasis original). Like Jesus' sacrifice on the cross, the Mass unites us intimately with Christ, separates us from sin, and unifies us as one body (see *CCC*, 1391–

1396). It has the same offering and the same priest—Jesus Christ: "At its [the Eucharistic assembly's] head is Christ himself, the principal agent of the Eucharist. He is high priest of the New Covenant; it is he himself who presides invisibly over every Eucharistic celebration" (*CCC*, 1348).

But there is a difference in the way the sacrifice is offered. Jesus only died and shed his blood once, but during the Mass, the glorified and risen Christ continues to offer himself and what he has accomplished on the cross to the Father for the sins of the world. This sacrifice, transcending time and space, is renewed and re-presented to God at every Mass.

Every time we attend Mass, we are active participants, playing a vital role. When the priest says, "Pray, brothers and sisters, that my sacrifice and yours may be acceptable to God, the almighty Father," and we say, "May the Lord accept the sacrifice at your hands, for the praise and glory of his name, for our good and the good of all his holy Church," we unite ourselves to the holy sacrifice of the Mass. What does that mean exactly? When we say the above response, we are offering our lives—our every word, thought, and action—along with the sacrifice of Jesus, to God the Father. We are offering ourselves to God, in union with the greatest sacrifice of all!

And now we get to receive Jesus in the Holy Eucharist! Partaking in the Eucharist makes us one with God and one with each other.[8] Without the Eucharist, we cannot live. Keeping a distance from the Eucharist or receiving the Eucharist unworthily can lead to spiritual death:

 Therefore whoever eats the bread or drinks the cup of the Lord unworthily will have to answer for the body and blood of the Lord. . . . For anyone who eats and drinks without discerning the body, eats and drinks judgment on himself. That is why many among you are ill and infirm, and a considerable number are dying. (1 Corinthians 11:27, 29-30)

Thus it is important to be free of mortal sin when receiving Communion; going to confession beforehand may be necessary. Also, as St. Paul says, we must recognize the Eucharist as "the body of the Lord," which is why the Church does not offer Communion to those who do not profess the Catholic faith, including the teaching of transubstantiation.

Some people might think it is enough to just pray to Jesus, since he is everywhere, rather than attend Mass on Sunday. But imagine yourself at home while your spouse is on a business trip. You can call and text them, but does any form of communication compare to physically being with them? Jesus is *truly* present at the Catholic Mass, and when we receive Communion, we make physical contact with him.[9] We become part of him, and he transforms us. "Whoever eats my flesh and drinks my blood remains in me and I in him" (John 6:56). "Remain in me, as I remain in you" (John 15:4).

When we leave Mass, we are more like Jesus, more the person he wants us to be, than we were when we came in. We are completely us—a purified version of ourselves, further removed from sin and closer to God. The Mass transforms us through the real presence of Christ. A sacrifice of love, it makes us "a community of love."[10]

This is my commandment: love one another as I love you. No one has greater love than this, to lay down one's life for one's friends. You are my friends if you do what I command you. I no longer call you slaves, because a slave does not know what his master is doing. I have called you friends, because I have told you everything I have heard from my Father. It was not you who chose me, but I who chose you and appointed you to go and bear fruit that will remain, so that whatever you ask the Father in my name he may give you. This I command you: love one another. (John 15:12-17)

What a blessing it is that, in our country, we can attend Mass every day, openly and without persecution. We have the privilege of participating in this profound miracle every day. Visit **Masstimes.org** to see the Masses in your area. Go offer your life to God, and receive Jesus Christ, who eagerly desires you!

MASS RESPONSES

Greeting
PRIEST: The Lord be with you.
PEOPLE: And with your spirit.

Penitential Act
Form A (Confiteor):
I confess to almighty God and to you, my brothers and sisters, that I have greatly sinned, in my thoughts and in my words, in what I have done and in what I have failed to do, through my fault, through my fault, through my most grievous fault; therefore I ask blessed Mary ever-Virgin, all the Angels and Saints, and you, my brothers and sisters, to pray for me to the Lord our God.

Form C (which may be sung):
PRIEST: Lord, have mercy.
PEOPLE: Lord, have mercy.

PRIEST: Christ, have mercy.
PEOPLE: Christ, have mercy.

PRIEST: Lord, have mercy.
PEOPLE: Lord, have mercy.

The Gloria
(on Sundays and many feast days, recited or sung)

Glory to God in the highest, and on earth peace to people of good will.

We praise you, we bless you, we adore you, we glorify you, we give you thanks for your great glory, Lord God, heavenly King, O God, almighty Father.

Lord Jesus Christ, Only Begotten Son, Lord God, Lamb of God, Son of the Father, you take away the sins of the world, have mercy on us; you take away the sins of the world, receive our prayer; you are seated at the right hand of the Father, have mercy on us.

For you alone are the Holy One, you alone are the Lord, you alone are the Most High, Jesus Christ, with the Holy Spirit, in the glory of God the Father. Amen.

Liturgy of the Word
First/Second Reading:
Lector: The Word of the Lord.
PEOPLE: Thanks be to God.

Gospel Dialogue:
PRIEST: The Lord be with you.
PEOPLE: And with your spirit.

PRIEST: A reading from the holy Gospel according to...
PEOPLE: Glory to you, O Lord.

PRIEST: The Gospel of the Lord.
PEOPLE: Praise to you, Lord Jesus Christ.

Profession of Faith
(Nicene Creed, on Sundays and some feasts and holy days)

I believe in one God, the Father almighty, maker of heaven and earth, of all things visible and invisible.

I believe in one Lord Jesus Christ, the Only Begotten Son of God, born of the Father before all ages. God from God, Light from Light, true God from true God, begotten, not made, consubstantial with the Father; through him all things were made. For us men and for our salvation he came down from heaven, [all bow] and by the Holy Spirit was incarnate of the Virgin Mary, and became man. [raise head]

For our sake he was crucified under Pontius Pilate, he suffered death and was buried, and rose again on the third day in accordance with the Scriptures.

Profession of Faith Cont.
He ascended into heaven and is seated at the right hand of the Father. He will come again in glory to judge the living and the dead and his kingdom will have no end.

I believe in the Holy Spirit, the Lord, the giver of life, who proceeds from the Father and the Son, who with the Father and the Son is adored and glorified, who has spoken through the prophets.

I believe in one, holy, catholic, and apostolic Church. I confess one Baptism for the forgiveness of sins and I look forward to the resurrection of the dead and the life of the world to come. Amen.

Prayers of the Faithful
LECTOR: Let us pray to the Lord.
PEOPLE: Lord, hear our prayer.
(Response may vary.)

Liturgy of the Eucharist
Invitation to Prayer:
PRIEST: Pray, brethren, that my sacrifice and yours may be acceptable to God, the almighty Father.
PEOPLE: May the Lord accept the sacrifice at your hands
for the praise and glory of his name, for our good and the good of all his holy Church.

Preface Dialogue:
PRIEST: The Lord be with you.
PEOPLE: And with your spirit.

PRIEST: Lift up your hearts.
PEOPLE: We lift them up to the Lord.

PRIEST: Let us give thanks to the Lord our God.
PEOPLE: It is right and just.

Priest reads the preface, after which the acclamation is recited or sung:
Holy, Holy, Holy Lord God of hosts. Heaven and earth are full of your glory. Hosanna in the highest. Blessed is he who comes in the name of the Lord. Hosanna in the highest.

Sometimes in Latin:
Sanctus, Sanctus, Sanctus Dominus Deus Sabaoth. Pleni sunt cæli et terra gloria tua. Hosanna in excelsis. Benedictus qui venit in nomine Domini. Hosanna in excelsis.

After the consecration, the priest invites us to acclaim "The Mystery of Faith." He recites the first few words, so we know which form to use.

PRIEST: Let us proclaim the mystery of faith.

All:

Form A: We proclaim your death, O Lord, and profess your resurrection until you come again.

Form B: When we eat this Bread and drink this Cup, we proclaim your death, O Lord, until you come again.

Form C: Save us, Savior of the world, for by your cross and resurrection, you have set us free.

The Great Amen
PRIEST: Through him, with him, and in him, in the unity of the Holy Spirit, all glory and honor is yours, almighty Father, for ever and ever.
PEOPLE: Amen. (Often sung)

The Lord's Prayer
PRIEST: Let us pray ...
PEOPLE: Our Father (page 135)

PRIEST: Deliver us, Lord, ... as we wait in joyful hope for the coming of our Savior, Jesus Christ.
PEOPLE: For the kingdom, the power, and the glory are yours now and forever.

Sign of Peace
PRIEST: The peace of the Lord be with you always.
PEOPLE: And with your spirit.

Lamb of God
Lamb of God, you take away the sins of the world, have mercy on us.

Lamb of God, you take away the sins of the world, have mercy on us.

Lamb of God, you take away the sins of the world, grant us peace.

Sometimes in Latin:
Agnus Dei, qui tollis peccata mundi, miserere nobis.

Agnus Dei, qui tollis peccata mundi, miserere nobis.

Agnus Dei, qui tollis peccata mundi, dona nobis pacem.

Invitation to Communion

PRIEST: Behold the Lamb of God, behold him who takes away the sins of the world. Blessed are those called to the supper of the Lamb.

PEOPLE: Lord, I am not worthy that you should enter under my roof, but only say the word and my soul shall be healed.

Concluding Rites

PRIEST: The Lord be with you.
PEOPLE: And with your spirit.

PRIEST: Go forth, the Mass is ended. *or* Go and announce the Gospel of the Lord. *or* Go in peace, glorifying the Lord by your life. *or* Go in peace.
PEOPLE: Thanks be to God

SUGGESTED READING

- *A Biblical Walk Through The Mass: Understanding What We Say And Do In The Liturgy*, Edward Sri.

- *God Is Near Us: The Eucharist, the Heart of Life,* Joseph Cardinal Ratzinger (Pope Benedict XVI).

- *Jesus and the Jewish Roots of the Eucharist: Unlocking the Secrets of the Last Supper*, Brant Pitre.

- *The Lamb's Supper: The Mass as Heaven on Earth,* Scott Hahn.

- *Magnificat* (us.magnificat.net) and *The Word Among Us* (wau.org) are monthly publications that give the Mass readings for each day, the prayers of the Mass, and inspiring meditations.

6

MARY, SAINTS, AND ANGELS

Behold, your mother.

John 19:27

The Virgin Mary: Mother of God, and Our Mother

We have a tender and loving mother in heaven, who watches over us and helps lead us to a close union with her Son. Jesus gave his mother to us:

 Then [Jesus] said to the disciple, "Behold, your mother." And from that hour the disciple took her into his home. (John 19:27)

"The disciple" in this passage is "whoever does the will of [the] heavenly Father" (Matthew 12:50). Jesus commands us to lovingly take Mary as our own mother. Catholics do not worship Mary; we honor and love her as she deserves to be honored and loved for her essential role in the salvation of man and for being a perfect example of living in God's will. Loving Mary as our mother and asking for her prayers magnifies our love for God.

From the deposit of faith Jesus Christ gave the Church, we know that Mary is the Mother of God, was a virgin throughout her whole life (perpetual virginity), was conceived without sin (Immaculate Conception), was assumed body and soul into heaven at the end of her earthly life (the Assumption), and is the Mother of the Church.

THE COMMUNION OF SAINTS

The communion of saints consists of the whole body of the Catholic Church, with Christ as the head. This includes faithful people on earth (the Church militant), in purgatory (the Church suffering), and in heaven (the Church triumphant). The support system of the communion of saints is invaluable in uniting us with God.

We have wonderful friends and allies in heaven, with the Virgin Mary being the most honored. These men and women have reached perfection—living in the presence of God and beholding his face—and they want nothing more than to help us achieve the same perfection. They love us and desire that we join them in heaven. Therefore it is important to ask for their prayers, as they are powerful intercessors on our behalf. God wants his people to help each other. He offers us the example of his children who have already completed their pilgrimage and are now home with him.

We are also called to pray for the souls still in purgatory. These are the departed who are in a final state of sanctification before entering the blessedness of heaven. (See more about purgatory in chapter 7, "Some Challenging Topics.") The Lord desires that his people "be perfect, just as your heavenly Father is perfect" (Matthew 5:48). We pray that these souls may enter the presence of God quickly. They are aware of our prayers for them and can offer prayers for us.

The most important thing in life is to love God and our neighbor with all our hearts (see Matthew 22:36-40). Helping ourselves and others reach God is the whole point of our existence. And this goal is possible by the graces God gives us through the sacraments, the spiritual gifts he gives us, our prayers, and the prayers of the faithful on earth, in purgatory, and in heaven. We are meant to be one big, loving and happy family, following God in all that we do.

ANGELS

Angels are real, and they are deeply involved in our daily lives (see *CCC*, 328-336). God created angels as pure spirits; they do not have material bodies as we do. He gave them free will and superior intelligence. Some angels proved faithful to God; others did not.

The angels who, through pride and envy, chose to revolt against God have permanently separated themselves from him. Fallen angels are referred to as demons, with Satan as their leader. Fallen angels try to tempt us into sin and to keep us as far away from God as possible.

The faithful angels are powerful messengers of God and allies for us in our struggle against evil. God gave each of us a guardian angel to guide and protect us throughout our earthly pilgrimage toward God and eternal life. We should take the time to thank our guardian angel daily!

Michael, Raphael, and Gabriel are mentioned in Scripture

as three of the archangels. God uses them for grand purposes: Michael contends against evil (see Daniel 10:13; Revelation 12:7); Raphael brings healing (see Tobit); and Gabriel announces the good news of God's salvation (see Daniel 9—10; Luke 1:11-38).

SUGGESTED READING

- *Angels of God: The Bible, the Church and the Heavenly Hosts*, Mike Aquilina.

- *Behold Your Mother: A Biblical and Historical Defense of the Marian Doctrines*, Tim Staples.

- *Hail, Holy Queen: The Mother of God in the Word of God,* Scott Hahn.

- *Saints: A Closer Look*, Fr. Thomas Dubay, SM.

- *Voices of the Saints: A Year of Readings*, Bert Ghezzi.

- *The World's First Love: Mary, Mother of God*, Abp. Fulton Sheen.

7
SOME CHALLENGING TOPICS

My grace is sufficient for you,
for power is made perfect in weakness.

2 Corinthians 12:9

SUFFERING

If God is perfect love and perfect goodness, why does he allow suffering? Sometimes God wants to heal the suffering caused by illness through prayer and the sacraments (see chapter 4, especially the section on the anointing of the sick). God's healing is a wonderful experience of his love and often a great sign to others of his reality and power.

Other suffering does not seem to yield to even the most fervent prayer. How do we reconcile such suffering with God's mercy and power?

The simple answer is that we can't, at least not fully. Our perspective is too small. It is only when we are face-to-face with God that we will understand how the big and small sufferings in the history of humanity helped shape God's perfect plan of love.

This is where trust comes in. We are called to put absolute faith in God, trusting that he works for our good in every situation. We might think of parents taking their young children to the doctor for their shots. These innocent babies cannot grasp the necessity of this painful experience. Even parents can find it difficult to put their children through this, but they know it is for a greater good, for their children's overall health and for the health of those around the child. Approaching pain and disappointment in this way, knowing that God the Father has the best possible intentions for us, his children, alleviates the worry and anxiety surrounding suffering.

We also need to remember that suffering is a result of original sin, and God is making good use of the mess original sin created. Even if we cannot see the meaning of our suffering, God can use it for our salvation, as well as for the salvation of others.

St. Paul the Apostle had an affliction that he prayed the Lord would relieve, and the Lord's response was, "My grace is sufficient for you, for power is made perfect in weakness" (2 Corinthians 12:9). St. Paul learned to embrace his suffering: "Now I rejoice in my sufferings for your sake, and in my flesh I am filling up what is lacking in the afflictions of Christ on behalf of his body, which is the church" (Colossians 1:24). Paul is not saying that Christ's sacrifice is insufficient; what can be lacking is our participation in his suffering for the salvation of the world. We can unite our sufferings to those of Jesus Christ for the good of ourselves and others—for the whole body of Christ, his Church!

We can't ignore the suffering in our lives and in our world. In all things we should turn to God, our Creator and Father, ask for his healing and help, and trust in the plan he has for us.

CHASTITY

What is chastity? A lot of people might think of it as simply celibacy, but that's not the only expression of it. Chastity is a virtue and a grace, and we are all called to be chaste, whether single or married (see *CCC*, 2348–2350).

Chastity is the interconnecting of our physical and spiritual sides, creating the perfect form of human sexuality—sexuality as God intended it. Chastity sustains our existence in the capacity of love and being, and it demands an integrity of the person along with an entire gift of self (see *CCC*, 2337–2347). When living a chaste life, a person experiences freedom, fulfillment, and growth, which invigorate and empower the person in every aspect of their lives. Imagine a symphony, its various parts combining and pouring forth one strong, impeccable melody. Through chastity we become the best version of ourselves.

Chastity is an imitation of Christ's purity. It involves self-mastery, which leads to freedom: "Either man governs his passions and finds peace, or he lets himself be dominated by them and becomes unhappy" (*CCC*, 2339). We are not meant to be slaves to our passions and desires. By way of grace and an act of our will, we choose what is good and rise to claim our dignity as human beings.

Through chastity, we give the gift of self to another. Chastity is expressed as friendship, whether of the same or opposite sex. The love and loyalty found in chaste friendships are a strong witness to God's fidelity and kindness (see *CCC*, 2346-2347).

Offenses against chastity include entertaining sexual thoughts, viewing pornography, masturbation, and *any* and *every* sexual act that separates the unitive and procreative elements of the sacred marriage act. Chastity leads us to deeper relationships with God and with others. St. Augustine wrote in his *Confessions*, "Indeed it is through chastity that we are gathered together and led back to the unity from which we were fragmented into multiplicity" (quoted in *CCC*, 2340).

The road to chastity is not an easy one; it can require constant vigilance and perseverance. We must remember that God is love. He loves each person deeply as a son or daughter; he loves us exactly how we are, right where we are. He loves us in this very moment, even in our brokenness and imperfection.

How do we react to unhealthy inclinations in the area of sexuality? The culture suggests the easy and wide road of following our desires. But St. Peter warns of the "worldly desires that wage war against the soul" (1 Peter 2:11). Jesus calls us to true freedom and discipleship: "Whoever wishes to come after me must deny himself, take up his cross, and follow me" (Matthew 16:24).

THE FOUR LAST THINGS: DEATH, JUDGMENT, HEAVEN, AND HELL

Because of original sin, the result of the fall of man, we all face physical death, which is the separation of the soul from the body (see Genesis 3:19). At the moment of death, we will be judged; this is called the particular judgment (see *CCC*, 1022). The general judgment will take place at the end of time, when Jesus comes again in glory and the righteous are reunited with their bodies in a glorified form.

Each person's faith journey is different. We cannot judge anyone's standing with God; only God knows what goes on inside the mind and heart. We can certainly pray for the deceased, and we trust in God's merciful love for each person.

Heaven is the place of perfect union with God, the Holy Trinity. It will be a state of never-ending love, happiness, and peace. There righteous souls will behold the glorious face of God.

Hell is reserved for souls who reject God. It is a place of complete separation from him.

Accepting the reality of heaven and hell is essential to our faith foundation. Through loving God and our fellow humans, we strive to be worthy of heaven and help others get there too. In turn, we must be aware of the reality of hell to avoid it, by rejecting sin and doing God's will.

When the Son of Man comes in his glory, and all the angels with him, he will sit upon his glorious throne, and all the nations will be assembled before him. And he will separate them one from another, as a shepherd separates the sheep from the goats.

He will place the sheep on his right and the goats on his left. Then the king will say to those on his right, "Come, you who are blessed by my Father. Inherit the kingdom prepared for you from the foundation of the world."

"For I was hungry and you gave me food, I was thirsty and you gave me drink, a stranger and you welcomed me, naked and you clothed me, ill and you cared for me, in prison and you visited me."

Then the righteous will answer him and say, "Lord, when did we see you hungry and feed you, or thirsty and give you drink? When did we see you a stranger and welcome you, or naked and clothe you? When did we see you ill or in prison, and visit you?"

And the king will say to them in reply, "Amen, I say to you, whatever you did for one of these least brothers of mine, you did for me."

Then he will say to those on his left, "Depart from me, you accursed, into the eternal fire prepared for the devil and his angels. For I was hungry and you gave me no food, I was thirsty and you gave me no drink, a stranger and you gave me no welcome, naked and you gave me no clothing, ill and in prison, and you did not care for me."

Then they will answer and say, "Lord, when did we see you hungry or thirsty or a stranger or naked or ill or in prison, and not minister to your needs?"

He will answer them, "Amen, I say to you, what you did not do for one of these least ones, you did not do for me." And these will go off to eternal punishment, but the righteous to eternal life. (Matthew 25:31-46)

PURGATORY

To enter heaven and behold the face of God, we must be in a state of perfect holiness. If we die in God's grace but without having our souls completely cleansed, we will go to purgatory, a state of final purification (see *CCC*, 1030-1031). The cleansing fire of purgatory, although probably not very pleasant, is sweetened by the certainty that we will reach God.

It is important to pray for loved ones and others who have passed away. Our prayers help them reach heaven faster, should they be undergoing purification in purgatory. Holy souls in purgatory know that we are praying for them, and once they arrive in heaven, they gratefully pray for our salvation.

The reality of purgatory is attested to in the Bible:

> [F]or no one can lay a foundation other than the one that is there, namely, Jesus Christ. If anyone builds on this foundation with gold, silver, precious stones, wood, hay, or straw, the work of each will come to light, for the Day will disclose it. It will be revealed with fire, and the fire [itself] will test the quality of each one's work. If the work stands that someone built upon the foundation, that person will receive a wage. But if someone's work is burned up, that

one will suffer loss; the person **will be saved, but only as through fire**. (1 Corinthians 3:11-15, emphasis added)

SPIRITUAL WARFARE IS REAL

Earth is a battleground of good and evil. Because of original sin, "the devil has acquired a certain domination over man, even though man remains free" (*CCC*, 407).

Man's original sin came through the seduction of Satan, the father of lies. He convinced man that he didn't need God and that he could be his own god. This seduction to sin, and more specifically to the sin of pride, is alive and well today. "Your opponent the devil is prowling around like a roaring lion looking for [someone] to devour" (1 Peter 5:8).

Many people in our society promote and even romanticize the occult, trying to make it seem harmless. It is not. Ghost hunting, astrology, New Age practices, magic, fortune telling, mediums, and more go against God's first commandment: "I am the Lord your God. . . . You shall not have other gods beside me" (Exodus 20:2-3). We must stay on the path God gave us and not fall victim to the wiles of the evil one.

God is stronger than the devil. Jesus gave us several examples of how to combat the evil one (see Mark 5:1-20; 9:14-29; Luke 4:1-13; 7:21). Catholic author Neal Lozano outlines five steps you can take each day to remain strong against Satan: repent and believe in Jesus, forgive anyone who has hurt you, renounce the evil one and his ways, take authority in Jesus' name over the evil one, and ask for the Father's blessing on all that you do.[11]

St. Michael the Archangel is a great warrior for us against the devil (see Revelation 12:7-8). The St. Michael Prayer, which many Catholics pray after Mass and after the rosary, is included in chapter 12, "Catholics Prayers."

MIRACLES

God has made his existence known throughout history in many ways, including miracles. In Scripture we see how he created everything out of nothing, parted the Red Sea for his people, and raised Jesus from the dead, to name just a few incidents (see Genesis 1; Exodus 14; Matthew 28). Our God is a God of power!

Scientifically proven miracles have continued through the ages of Christendom and across the world, often through the intercession of Mary and the saints. For example, the Blessed Virgin Mary appeared at Tepeyac, Mexico, under the name Santa María de Guadalupe, in the 1531 and left her image on the cloak of a poor native. Over ten million indigenous people were brought to Christ through this image, still viewed today at a large cathedral in Mexico City.

St. Padre Pio is a modern-day saint who experienced many miracles—bilocation, healing, words of knowledge and wisdom—all for the salvation of people and the glory of God.

SUGGESTED READING

- *Chastity Is for Lovers: Single, Happy, and (Still) a Virgin*, Arleen Spenceley.

- *The Four Last Things: A Catechetical Guide to Death, Judgment, Heaven, and Hell*, Fr. Wade L. J. Menezes, CPM.

- *Healing: Bringing the Gift of God's Mercy to the World,* Mary Healy.

- *Heaven Starts Now: Become a Saint Day by Day*, Fr. John Riccardo.

- *Made for Love: Same-Sex Attraction and the Catholic Church*, Michael Schmitz

- *Making Sense Out of Suffering*, Peter Kreeft.

- *Unbound: A Practical Guide to Deliverance*, Neal Lozano.

- *Why I Don't Call Myself Gay: How I Reclaimed My Sexual Reality and Found Peace*, Daniel Mattson.

8

LIFE ISSUES

*You formed my inmost being;
you knit me in my mother's womb.*
Psalm 139:13

LIFE IS A GIFT

Pope St. John Paul II reminds us of our responsibility regarding life in "Evangelium Vitae" ["The Gospel of Life"]:

[W]e are facing an enormous and dramatic clash between good and evil, death and life, the "culture of death" and the "culture of life." We find ourselves not only "faced with" but necessarily "in the midst of" this conflict: we are all involved and we all share in it, with the inescapable responsibility of choosing to be unconditionally pro-life.[12]

The most precious gift from God is life. Without that gift, we would not be here! God willed the creation of each of us out of love.

As our culture has shifted from a culture of life to a culture of death, it is imperative that we understand Catholic teachings on life and embrace them as Christ's plan for our complete happiness, peace, and freedom. These teachings offer the human person the dignity that God intends for those created in his image and likeness.

OPENNESS TO LIFE

God calls spouses to be open to life. When a man and a woman come together in the marriage act, two essential aspects must be preserved: the unitive and the procreative. The marriage act is unitive in that it is a true mutual love between spouses, and it is procreative in that it is ordered toward new life, the fruit and fulfillment of this mutual love.

In 1968 Pope Paul VI issued his encyclical letter "Humanae Vitae" ("Of Human Life"). He upheld the Church's traditional teaching that "each and every marital act must of necessity retain its intrinsic relationship to the procreation of human life. This particular doctrine . . . is based on the inseparable connection, established by God, which man on his own initiative may not break, between the unitive significance and the procreative significance which are both inherent to the marriage act."[13] Contraception removes the procreative element from the union.

The spouses' call to transmit human life requires "a sense of human and Christian responsibility" (*CCC*, 2367). Thus the Church allows married couples to discern the size of their families through natural methods referred to as Natural Family Planning:

 For just reasons, spouses may wish to space the births of

their children. It is their duty to make certain that their desire is not motivated by selfishness but is in conformity with the generosity appropriate to responsible parenthood. Moreover, they should conform their behavior to the objective criteria of morality. (*CCC*, 2368)

The Church's teaching runs counter to the norm in our society. It is a teaching steeped in tradition and sacred Scripture (see Genesis 1:28; 38:9-10; Psalm 127:3-5; 1 Timothy 2:15), which clearly reveal God's plan for humanity. Every Christian church condemned contraception until 1930, when the Anglican Church approved its use for certain cases. Today the Catholic Church is one of the few who hold true to the ancient Christian teaching on this issue.

What is perhaps looked upon as an old rule that is out of step with modern society is actually a pathway to love and freedom. Pope Paul VI predicted what would occur if contraception was embraced, and everything he warned about is happening: infidelity and moral decline, loss of respect for women, abuse of power by public authorities, and the belief that we should have unlimited dominion over our bodies and physical make-up.[14] The repair of these sufferings requires embracing our sexuality as intended by God. This is the key to the rebuilding of morality in our society.

EMBRACING LIFE FROM CONCEPTION TO NATURAL DEATH

God alone is the Lord of life from its beginning until its end: no one can under any circumstance claim for himself the right directly to destroy an innocent human being. (*CCC*, 2258)

Abortion

 Before I formed you in the womb I knew you, before you were born I dedicated you. (Jeremiah 1:5)

Abortion is gravely contrary to the moral law. This has been the consistent teaching of the Church since apostolic times.

The *Catechism* states that from the moment of conception, a human life must be protected and respected. At the point of existence, the moment of conception, the human being has the rights of a person, which include the right to life. Christian doctrine has always affirmed that direct abortion is "gravely contrary to the moral law," and this doctrine is "unchangeable" (see *CCC*, 2270-2271).

Euthanasia

The Catholic Dictionary, in its section on euthanasia, states:

 The Catholic Church reprobates euthanasia because it is a usurpation of God's lordship over human life. As creatures of God, to whom human beings owe every element of their existence, they are entrusted only with the stewardship of their earthly lives. They are bound to accept the life that God gave them, with its limitations and powers; to preserve this life as the first condition of their dependence on the Creator; and not deliberately curtail their time of probation on earth, during which they are to work out and thereby merit the happiness of their final destiny.[15]

Respect is owed to all human beings, with special care for those who are handicapped, sick, or dying. Directly causing one of these persons to die is morally unacceptable.

On the other hand, refusing or discontinuing medical treatments "that are burdensome, dangerous, extraordinary, or disproportionate to the expected outcome can be legitimate" (*CCC*, 2278). In these situations, the death of the person is not willed, and one simply accepts its imminence.

Even when a person is thought to be nearing death, ordinary care is due them. The use of pain medication to alleviate suffering, even if it might shorten a person's days, can be morally acceptable. Palliative care "should be encouraged" (*CCC*, 2279).

Suicide

We are all responsible for preserving the life God has given us; it is not ours to dispose of. We should consider our very existence with the utmost gratitude. Suicide is unnatural and contrary to the love of self, neighbor, and God. It severs ties with and neglects obligations to family, community, and nation (see *CCC*, 2280-2281).

It is important to note that severe psychological issues and dire situations can obstruct the responsibility of the person committing suicide:

> We should not despair of the eternal salvation of persons who have taken their own lives. By ways known to him alone, God can provide the opportunity for salutary repentance. The Church prays for persons who have taken their own lives. (*CCC*, 2283)

A Child Is a Gift, Not a Right

> A child is not something *owed* to one, but is a *gift*. The "supreme gift of marriage" is a new human person. A child

may not be considered a piece of property, an idea to which an alleged "right to a child" would lead. (*CCC*, 2378)

The Church acknowledges infertility as a tremendous suffering for a married couple and encourages morally acceptable research geared toward reducing human sterility. But any practices that make human life a commodity or that diminish human rights, the sanctity of marriage, or the dignity of the human person are prohibited, for example:

• The use of donors and surrogates violates the integrity of the marital relationship.

• Artificial insemination substitutes a technological procedure for the couple's loving sexual union.

• In vitro fertilization depersonalizes the act of generating a child and often involves the destruction of embryos.

God has a plan for each of our lives. "We know that all things work for good for those who love God, who are called according to his purpose" (Romans 8:28). The Church offers this encouragement to married couples:

The Gospel shows that physical sterility is not an absolute evil. Spouses who still suffer from infertility after exhausting legitimate medical procedures should unite themselves with the Lord's Cross, the source of all spiritual fecundity. They can give expression to their generosity by adopting abandoned children or performing demanding services for others. (*CCC*, 2379)

SUGGESTED READING

- "Humanae Vitae" ["Of Human Life"], Pope Paul VI (available at Vatican.va and other sites).

- *Men & Women Are from Eden: A Study Guide to John Paul II's Theology of the Body*, Mary Healy.

- *Persuasive Pro-Life*, Trent Horn.

- *Theology of the Body for Beginners: A Basic Introduction to Pope John Paul II's Sexual Revolution*, Revised Edition, Christopher West.

- "Reproductive Technology," United States Conference of Catholic Bishops (http://www.usccb.org/issues-and-action/human-life-and-dignity/reproductive-technology/index.cfm).

- *Unplanned: The Dramatic True Story of a Former Planned Parenthood Leader's Eye-Opening Journey Across the Life Line*, Abby Johnson.

9
WHAT MUST I DO?

*If you remain in my word, you will truly be my
disciples, and you will know the truth,
and the truth will set you free.*
John 8:31-32

OBEY GOD'S LAW

The Ten Commandments
1. I am the LORD your God: You shall not have strange gods before me.
2. You shall not take the name of the Lord your God in vain.
3. Remember to keep holy the Lord's Day.
4. Honor your father and mother.
5. You shall not kill.
6. You shall not commit adultery.
7. You shall not steal.

8. You shall not bear false witness against your neighbor.
9. You shall not covet your neighbor's wife.
10. You shall not covet your neighbor's goods.

(See Exodus 20:1-17; Deuteronomy 5:6-21)

The Great Commandment

> Jesus replied, "The first is this: 'Hear, O Israel! The Lord our God is Lord alone! You shall love the Lord your God with all your heart, with all your soul, with all your mind, and with all your strength.' The second is this: 'You shall love your neighbor as yourself.' There is no other commandment greater than these." (Mark 12:29-31)

The New Commandment

> Love one another. As I have loved you, so you also should love one another. (John 13:34)

Commandments of the Church (see *CCC*, 2041-2043)

1. To attend Mass on all Sundays and holy days of obligation.
2. To confess sins at least once a year.
3. To receive Holy Communion during the Easter season.
4. To fast and to abstain on the days appointed.
5. To contribute to the support of the Church.

Spiritual Works of Mercy

1. Instruct the ignorant.
2. Counsel the doubtful.
3. Admonish sinners.
4. Bear wrongs patiently.
5. Forgive offenses.
6. Console the afflicted.
7. Pray for the living and the dead.

Corporal Works of Mercy

1. Feed the hungry.
2. Shelter the homeless.
3. Clothe the naked.
4. Visit the sick.
5. Visit the imprisoned.
6. Bury the dead.
7. Give alms to the poor.

GROW IN VIRTUE

The Beatitudes

> Blessed are the poor in spirit, for theirs is the kingdom of heaven.
>
> Blessed are they who mourn, for they will be comforted.
>
> Blessed are the meek, for they will inherit the land.
>
> Blessed are they who hunger and thirst for righteousness, for they will be satisfied.

Blessed are the merciful, for they will be shown mercy.

Blessed are the clean of heart, for they will see God.

Blessed are the peacemakers, for they will be called children of God.

Blessed are they who are persecuted for the sake of righteousness, for theirs is the kingdom of heaven.

(Matthew 5:3-10)

Cardinal Virtues

These four virtues are central in the Christian life and are therefore called "cardinal" (see *CCC*, 1805).

1. **Prudence** disposes us toward good and enables us to choose the good.

2. **Justice** disposes us to give God and our neighbor what is due them.

3. **Fortitude** gives us strength in pursuing good in spite of difficulties.

4. **Temperance** helps us moderate our attractions to pleasure.

Theological Virtues

The theological virtues relate directly to God. They dispose Christians to live in a relationship with the Holy Trinity. They have the One and Triune God for their origin, motive, and object. (*CCC*, 1812)

1. **Faith** is the virtue by which we believe in God and his revelation.

2. **Hope** is the virtue by which we aspire toward heaven, placing all our trust in God.

3. **Charity/Love** is the virtue by which we love God and love our neighbor.

The Seven Capital Sins and the Seven Capital Virtues

Capital Sin	Capital Virtue (Conquers Capital Sin)
Pride	Humility
Greed	Generosity
Lust	Chastity
Envy	Kindness
Gluttony	Temperance
Anger	Patience
Sloth	Diligence

BE OPEN TO THE HOLY SPIRIT

The Gifts of the Holy Spirit (see *CCC*, 1831)

1. Wisdom
2. Understanding
3. Counsel
4. Fortitude
5. Knowledge
6. Piety
7. Fear of the Lord

The Fruits of the Holy Spirit (see *CCC*, 1832; Galatians 5:22-23)

1. Charity
2. Joy
3. Peace
4. Patience
5. Kindness
6. Goodness
7. Generosity
8. Gentleness
9. Faithfulness
10. Modesty
11. Self-control
12. Chastity

SUGGESTED READING

- *Beatitudes: Eight Steps to Happiness*, Raniero Cantalamessa, OFM Cap.

- *The Four Loves*, C. S. Lewis.

- *The Imitation of Christ*, Thomas à Kempis.

- *Introduction to the Devout Life*, St. Francis de Sales.

- *Mere Christianity*, C. S. Lewis.

- *Story of a Soul*, St. Thérèse of Lisieux.

- *Walk Humbly with Your God: Simple Steps to a Virtuous Life*, Fr. Andrew Apostoli, CFR.

10

LIVING THE FULLNESS OF THE CATHOLIC FAITH

This is the will of God, your holiness.
1 Thessalonians 4:3

God created us as unique individuals with specific gifts to sanctify us and help others get to heaven. He has chosen each of us to live forever with him, to achieve holiness, and to be saints! How can we accept his invitation? Here are five *P*s for growing in perfection.

PRAY

We must ask Jesus, through the power of the Holy Spirit, to touch our hearts, to help us understand the truth of God, and to lead us in carrying out his will. We should talk to God as we would to a friend—with sincerity, telling him our worries, our sins, and how we are feeling. Also, we should take the time daily to pray and meditate on the Word of God. When we take this time to pray—and this includes listening to God in silence—a relationship is formed. This personal relationship with God is key to our happiness and fulfillment.

We are never alone because God is always with us. Yet prayer can feel difficult. Sometimes we must push through our feelings and continue to seek God.

God will never force his way into our lives; we need to invite him in. He is with us right now and is waiting for us to acknowledge him, to accept his embrace and his love. That love is real and powerful.

PREPARE

The Church offers us many ways to prepare for a deeper union with God. There might be sins in our lives that block us from knowing, loving, and serving God. Before receiving Jesus Christ in the Holy Eucharist, we want to be sure we are in line with God's will. The sacrament of reconciliation, or confession (see chapter 4), is a place to encounter our merciful God. He is waiting with loving arms to embrace us and give us his grace.

If you use contraceptives, are a baptized Catholic married outside the Church, are sexually active outside of marriage, or are otherwise out of line with Church teachings, seek the counsel of a good priest. A priest can also guide you in completing your sacramental preparation. The Rite of Christian Initiation for Adults (RCIA) is the first step toward becoming a Catholic. Attending RCIA is beneficial for both non-Catholics and lapsed Catholics. Simply call any local Catholic parish to inquire about their RCIA program. If we sincerely want to live in union with God, God will help us get on the right path.

Nothing is more important than our salvation. We must realize the way God wants us to live, and then take the necessary steps to adjust our lives. This might seem difficult, depending on our circumstances, but God will bless us enormously.

 Trust in the LORD with all your heart, on your own intelligence do not rely; In all your ways be mindful of him, and he will make straight your paths. (Proverbs 3:5-6)

It doesn't matter if it has been fifty years since your last confession; God is waiting for you. Don't hold back sins because of embarrassment or fear. The priest hears thousands of confessions, and nothing will shock him. He is Christ's representative in offering pardon and absolution. Confession is between us and God.

Before going to confession, examine your conscience, asking for God's help. Here is one examination that might be helpful, based on the Ten Commandments:

1. I am the Lord your God: You shall not have strange gods before me.

Do you put God first in your life? Or have you put money, material things, or other people before God?

2. You shall not take the name of the Lord your God in vain.

Have you used God's name in anger or jest?

3. Remember to keep holy the Lord's Day.

Have you attended Mass every Sunday and on holy days of obligation? Have you kept Sunday as a day for rest and spiritual activities, not work?

4. Honor your father and mother.

Have you been respectful to your parents and all legitimate authority figures in your life?

5. You shall not kill.

Have you had an abortion or helped someone obtain an abortion? Have you killed someone emotionally with your anger and verbal abuse? Have you damaged your own body through excesses in food or drink, laziness, or lack of sleep?

6. You shall not commit adultery.

Have you engaged in any sins of the flesh? This includes entertaining sexual thoughts, masturbation, sexual acts outside of marriage, watching or reading pornography, and using contraception.

7. You shall not steal.

Have you taken something from someone? Have you wasted time at work?

8. You shall not bear false witness against your neighbor.

Have you lied, gossiped, or embellished the truth?

9. You shall not covet your neighbor's wife.

Have you failed to give all love and attention to your spouse?

10. You shall not covet your neighbor's goods.

Are you happy and grateful to God for what you have? Are you happy for the well-being of others?

PARTICIPATE

We might think that we can be close to God on our own terms, separate from a church community. But "Jesus and me" is not the Church Christ founded. A vibrant Catholic community will strengthen our union with God.

 We should not stay away from our assembly, as is the custom of some, but encourage one another, and this all the more as you see the day drawing near. (Hebrews 10:25)

Obey your leaders and defer to them, for they keep watch over you and will have to give an account, that they may fulfill their task with joy and not with sorrow, for that would be of no advantage to you. (Hebrews 13:17)

It is good to register at a local parish, where you can attend Mass, receive the sacraments, and develop supportive relationships with other Catholics.

PRACTICE

"Go and announce the Gospel of the Lord." "Glorify the Lord by your life." These are the parting words at Mass. Jesus wants us to lead people to God, and we do this by word and example.

We can practice our faith by being Jesus Christ to others. He calls us to love people—all people. We give ourselves to God when we serve our spouse, kids, family, and community. God calls us to selfless and merciful love.

We can learn from experienced Catholic evangelists how to explain our faith delicately and humbly. Each of us has spiritual gifts, and there are programs that can help uncover those gifts and show us how to use them to build the kingdom.

PERSEVERE

On our faith journey, we will meet trials, temptations, and apparent roadblocks. We must not give up! If we keep our eyes on Jesus, we can push through each obstacle that comes up. We can turn to Jesus and ask for guidance. This process is like training to be an Olympic athlete.

 Every athlete exercises discipline in every way. They do it to win a perishable crown, but we an imperishable one. (1 Corinthians 9:25)

A LIVELY CATHOLIC'S TO-DO LIST

- Pray regularly. Start with fifteen minutes a day and work up to more, even an hour.

- Read the Bible. You can download Catholic Daily Readings App, join a Catholic Bible study, or read a little every day on your own.

- Attend Mass and receive Holy Communion every Sunday and on holy days of obligation. Go to daily Mass too if you can.

- Meet with a priest and discuss ways to get your life in line with God.

- Receive the sacrament of reconciliation at least once a year, preferably monthly or more frequently.

- Register at a local parish.

- Pray the rosary, alone or with others, weekly or even daily.

- Fast: deny yourself things you are attached to, such as food, sweets, television, internet.

- Learn about your faith. Read the *Catechism of the Catholic Church* and books suggested here; listen to Catholic radio and watch Catholic TV (EWTN), attend Catholic conferences, lectures, and retreats.

- Spend time in adoration before the Blessed Sacrament.

- Take a spiritual gifts class to discover what gifts you have and how to use them. Catherine of Siena Institute offers Called & Gifted (see siena.org/called-gifted).

- Read your parish bulletin, take classes, go to events, and join groups that interest you.

- Give money as you are able, to support your parish and other Christian initiatives.

- Review and realign your priorities in life: 1) God, 2) Spouse, 3) Children ….

May the God of peace himself make you perfectly holy and may you entirely, spirit, soul, and body, be preserved blameless for the coming of our Lord Jesus Christ.

1 Thessalonians 5:23

SUGGESTED READING

- *Contemplative Provocations: Brief, Concentrated Observations on Aspects of a Life with God*, Fr. Donald Haggerty.

- *Five Pillars of the Spiritual Life: A Practical Guide to Prayer for Active People*, Fr. Robert Spitzer, SJ.

- *An Ignatian Introduction to Prayer: Scriptural Reflections According to the "Spiritual Exercises"*, Fr. Timothy M. Gallagher, OMV.

- *St. Joseph Guide to the Bible: Becoming Comfortable with the Bible in Four Simple Steps*, Karl A. Schultz.

- *33 Days to Morning Glory: A Do-It-Yourself Retreat In Preparation for Marian Consecration*, Fr. Michael E. Gaitley, MIC.

- *You Did It to Me: A Practical Guide to Mercy in Action*, Fr. Michael E. Gaitley, MIC.

11

CATHOLIC PRACTICES: HOW AND WHY

Stand firm and hold fast to the traditions that you were taught.
2 Thessalonians 2:15

The Church offers many unique practices to help us grow in holiness. Some of these practices will be explained in this chapter.

EUCHARISTIC ADORATION

Many Catholic churches have an adoration chapel, where Jesus Christ is present in the Blessed Sacrament in a special way. As we discussed in chapters 4 and 5, when the priest consecrates the host, the true presence—body, blood, soul, and divinity—of Jesus

Christ becomes present. Adoration of the Eucharist is being with Jesus and is the next closest thing to receiving him sacramentally.

In the adoration chapel, the Blessed Sacrament is exposed in a windowed container called a monstrance. Because we are coming before Jesus, the utmost reverence is required. It is customary to genuflect or kneel upon entering and exiting the chapel.

We can do many things in an adoration chapel, such as pray the rosary or chaplets, spiritual reading, spiritual writing, sitting in silence listening to God, personal prayer, set prayers. The important thing is to be with God. Some parishes have prayer groups that meet in the chapel to pray together. Going to these groups and having times of quiet prayer are both wonderful experiences.

There are many accounts of profound encounters with Jesus in Eucharistic adoration. Pope St. John Paul II describes his experience:

> It is pleasant to spend time with him, to lie close to his breast like the Beloved Disciple (cf. John 13:25) and to feel the infinite love present in his heart. . . . [H]ow can we not feel a renewed need to spend time in spiritual converse, in silent adoration, in heartfelt love before Christ present in the Most Holy Sacrament?[16]

GENUFLECTION

In most Catholic churches, a tabernacle containing the Holy Eucharist is near the altar. A burning red candle signals the presence of Jesus Christ. When entering and exiting a pew or passing in front of the tabernacle, Catholics genuflect—that is, they bow down and touch the right knee to the floor. A double genuflection, kneeling on both knees, is often done before the Blessed Sacrament exposed in a monstrance. Some Catholics genuflect before or while receiving the Holy Eucharist, but most people simply bow the head in reverence.

SACRAMENTALS

Sacramentals are objects or actions that carry God's blessing and bring us to a more profound relationship with Christ. They extend the grace of the sacraments into everything that we do. Examples of sacramentals are holy water, rosaries, religious medals, the sign of the cross, and the Liturgy of the Hours. Sacramentals are not good luck charms and should not be used in a superstitious way.

THE SIGN OF THE CROSS

According to the writings of St. Basil (fourth century), the sign of the cross comes from the time of the apostles and was administered in baptisms.[17] Overtime it evolved into the sign of the cross we know today.

Roman Catholics touch the index and middle fingers of the right hand to their forehead, saying, "In the name of the Father," to the chest, "and of the Son," to the left and then the right shoulder, "and of the Holy Spirit," and then they bring the hands together in prayer, "Amen."

Making the sign of the cross is a powerful prayer. We invoke the Father, the Son, and the Holy Spirit, coming into the presence of the Triune God. We also acknowledge the cross as the source of our redemption.

The sign of the cross is a sacramental. By making it reverently, we renew our baptismal vows and link to the Body of Christ. It states that we belong to Christ and follow Christ in all things, as his disciples. We accept our participation in Christ's suffering. It is a strong defense against the devil, for by it we proclaim that Christ is our protection and that we belong to him. Making the sign of the cross during times of trial can alleviate distress and prevent our falling into sin and self-indulgence.[18]

Though Catholics make the sign of the cross frequently, it is important that we not take it lightly. This sign draws on the prayer of the Catholic Church, the Body of Christ. It acknowledges that everything we do, we do in the presence of God.

HOLY WATER

Holy water, water that has been blessed by a priest or deacon, is a powerful sacramental, consistently found in baptismal fonts and at the entrances of Catholic churches. Upon entering and exiting a church, it is customary to dip our fingers in the holy water and make the sign of the cross. This signifies a renewal of our baptismal vows, in which we reject sin and Satan and profess the beliefs of the Catholic Church as found in the Creed. Many Catholics keep holy water in their homes and use it in blessing themselves and others and as protection against evil.

THE ROSARY

The rosary is one of the most powerful prayers God has given us. To put it simply, the rosary is prayerful meditation on key moments in the life of Jesus Christ. These twenty mysteries from sacred Scripture are referred to as the joyful, luminous, sorrowful, and glorious mysteries. Most people pray one set of these mysteries at a time. We meditate through the lens of Jesus' mother and ours, Mary. We can imagine her taking our hand and leading us through the events of Christ's life, drawing us ever closer to her Son.

In chapter 12, "Catholic Prayers," I give more detail on how to pray the rosary and have included all the mysteries. Praying the rosary is more than saying the words and moving the beads through your fingers; what is important is to be attentive in your heart to the mysteries of Christ's life.

Some people pray the rosary while driving or working out; others kneeling in front of the Blessed Sacrament. The rosary helps us enter more fully into the life of Christ. It has been instrumental throughout Christian history in defeating the powers of evil. It has been called the spiritual weapon of our time.

FASTING AND ABSTINENCE

Because of original sin, we are inclined toward self-indulgence. By fasting or practicing self-denial, we can break free from this sinful inclination, get closer to God in prayer, and hear his voice more clearly.

There are two days in the year, Ash Wednesday and Good Friday, when Catholics between the ages of eighteen and fifty-nine are required to fast, and all over the age of thirteen must abstain from meat. On these days, the typical practice is to eat one regular, meatless meal in addition to two smaller meatless meals that together do not equal one meal.

Not everyone will fast in the same way. Some Catholics eat only plain bread and drink water or juice. A person who does heavy labor and needs to eat a lot for strength might practice other forms of self-denial, such as listening to Catholic radio instead of secular music, skipping milk and sugar in their coffee, or eating plain toast instead of a sweet pastry. Similarly, the aged, the sick, and pregnant and nursing mothers can find methods of self-denial appropriate to their current state.

The first requirement of fasting and self-denial is that they be done for love of God. Even one act of self-denial every day can bring surprising fruit to our lives. Self-denial can make us grateful for the little things we enjoy. It helps us see how much we are blessed and how God is present in every moment and behind every one of our blessings. Self-denial also builds in us the virtue of humility, as we depend on God for sustenance and joy apart from earthly pleasures.

RELICS

Relics are material objects associated with saints. Through relics of the saints, God extends his grace and power in the case of miraculous healings. Relics can inspire us to turn our attention to the saints as models and intercessors.

Relics are not magic and do not contain any power separate from God. All good coming about through a relic is from God. Relics are of the following categories:

- first-class relics: parts of the body of a saint, such as bone, hair, and skin;

- second-class relics: items used by a saint, such as articles of clothing, rosaries, and books;

- third-class relics: items that a saint touched or that have been touched to a first-, second-, or another third-class relic, with the intention of their becoming third-class relics.

Thousands of miraculous healings coming through the relics of saints have been documented. Here is one account in Scripture:

 And so Elisha died and was buried.

> At that time of year, bands of Moabites used to raid the land. Once some people were burying a man, when suddenly they saw such a raiding band. So they cast the man into the grave of Elisha, and everyone went off. But when the man came in contact with the bones of Elisha, he came back to life and got to his feet. (2 Kings 13:20-21)

The proper way to venerate a relic is with a sincere and humble heart, open to God's love. Relics are often contained in ornate containers called reliquaries, which we can touch with our hands or with an item of devotion. Common practices also include touching the relic to the forehead, kissing the hand and then touching the relic, and kissing the relic itself. Any respectful action is appropriate if our intent is to experience God's love through the relics of his saints.

Most parishes have relics, and Father Carlos Martins, CC, brings an extensive collection of relics to parishes across the country through the evangelization apostolate Treasures of the Church (Treasuresofthechurch.com).

I praise you because you remember me in everything and hold fast to the traditions, just as I handed them on to you.

1 Corinthians 11:2

SUGGESTED READING

- *Champions of the Rosary: The History and Heroes of a Spiritual Weapon*, Fr. Donald H. Calloway, MIC.

- *The Sign of the Cross: Recovering the Power of the Ancient Prayer*, Bert Ghezzi.

- *Why Do Catholics Genuflect? And Answers to Other Puzzling Questions About the Catholic Church*, Al Kresta.

12
CATHOLIC PRAYERS

Pray without ceasing.
1 Thessalonians 5:17

ESSENTIAL PRAYERS

Our Father

Our Father, who art in heaven, hallowed be thy name; thy kingdom come; thy will be done on earth as it is in heaven. Give us this day our daily bread; and forgive us our trespasses, as we forgive those who trespass against us; and lead us not into temptation, but deliver us from evil. Amen.

Hail Mary

Hail Mary, full of grace, the Lord is with thee; blessed art thou among women, and blessed is the fruit of thy womb, Jesus. Holy Mary, Mother of God, pray for us sinners now and at the hour of our death. Amen.

Glory Be

Glory be to the Father, and to the Son, and to the Holy Spirit; as it was in the beginning, is now, and ever shall be, world without end. Amen.

Nicene Creed

I believe in one God, the Father almighty, maker of heaven and earth, of all things visible and invisible.

I believe in one Lord Jesus Christ, the Only Begotten Son of God, born of the Father before all ages. God from God, Light from Light, true God from true God, begotten, not made, consubstantial with the Father; through him all things were made.

For us men and for our salvation he came down from heaven, (bow) and by the Holy Spirit was incarnate of the Virgin Mary, and became man. (raise head) For our sake he was crucified under Pontius Pilate, he suffered death and was buried, and rose again on the third day in accordance with the Scriptures.

He ascended into heaven and is seated at the right hand of the Father. He will come again in glory to judge the living and the dead, and his kingdom will have no end.

I believe in the Holy Spirit, the Lord, the giver of life, who proceeds from the Father and the Son, who with the Father and the Son is adored and glorified, who has spoken through the prophets.

I believe in one, holy, catholic, and apostolic Church. I confess one Baptism for the forgiveness of sins, and I look forward to the resurrection of the dead and the life of the world to come. Amen.

Apostles' Creed

I believe in God, the Father almighty, Creator of heaven and earth, and in Jesus Christ, his only Son, our Lord, who was conceived by the Holy Spirit, born of the Virgin Mary, suffered under Pontius Pilate, was crucified, died, and was buried; he descended into hell; on the third day he rose again from the dead; he ascended into heaven, and is seated at the right hand of God the Father almighty; from there he will come to judge the living and the dead.

I believe in the Holy Spirit, the holy catholic Church, the communion of saints, the forgiveness of sins, the resurrection of the body, and life everlasting. Amen.

Spiritual Communion

When we cannot receive Holy Communion—because of illness keeping us from Mass or a need for confession, for example—the following prayer or one like it can be a source of grace and unite us with the Lord's sacrifice.

My Jesus, I believe that you are present in the Most Holy Sacrament. I love you above all things, and I desire to receive you into my soul. Since I cannot at this moment receive you sacramentally, come at least spiritually into my heart. I embrace you as if you were already there and unite myself wholly to you. Never permit me to be separated from you. Amen.

Jesus Prayer

Lord Jesus Christ, Son of God, have mercy on me, a sinner.

Angelus

Traditionally said at 6am, 12pm, and 6pm, this beautiful prayer celebrating the Incarnation can be said at any time of day. If you attend Mass at these times you might notice the Angelus is prayed all together before Mass begins.

V. The angel of the Lord declared unto Mary,
R. And she conceived of the Holy Spirit.
Hail Mary, full of grace, the Lord is with thee;
blessed art thou among women,
and blessed is the fruit of thy womb, Jesus.
Holy Mary, Mother of God, pray for us sinners,
now and at the hour of our death. Amen.

V. Behold the handmaid of the Lord.
R. Be it done unto me according to thy word.
Hail Mary . . .

V. And the Word was made flesh (all genuflect)
R. And dwelt among us.
Hail Mary . . .

V. Pray for us, O Holy Mother of God,
R. That we may be made worthy of the promises of Christ.

V. Let us pray.
Pour forth, we beseech thee, O Lord, thy grace into our hearts; that we to whom the incarnation of Christ thy Son was made known by the message of an angel, may by his passion and cross be brought to the glory of his resurrection, through the same Christ Our Lord. Amen.

St. Michael the Archangel Prayer
St. Michael the Archangel, defend us in battle. Be our protection against the wickedness and snares of the devil. May God rebuke him, we humbly pray, and do thou, O Prince of the heavenly hosts, by the power of God, cast into hell Satan and all the evil spirits who prowl about the world seeking the ruin of souls. Amen.

Prayer to My Guardian Angel
Angel of God, my guardian dear, to whom God's love commits me here, ever this day, be at my side, to light and guard, to rule and guide. Amen.

An Act of Contrition
O my God, I am heartily sorry for having offended thee, and I detest all my sins because of thy just punishments, but most of all because they offend thee, my God, who art all good and deserving of all my love. I firmly resolve, with the help of thy grace, to sin no more and to avoid the near occasions of sin. Amen.

A Prayer to the Holy Spirit
O Holy Spirit, Beloved of my soul, I adore you. Enlighten, guide, strengthen, and console me. Tell me what I ought to say and do, and command me to do it. I promise to be submissive in everything that you ask of me and to accept all that you permit to happen to me; only show me what is your will. Amen.

Morning Offerings
O my God, in union with the Immaculate Heart of Mary, I offer thee the Precious Blood of Jesus from all the altars throughout the

world, joining with it the offering of my every thought, word, and action of this day. O my Jesus, I desire today to gain every indulgence and merit I can, and I offer them, together with myself, to Mary Immaculate, that she may best apply them to the interests of thy most Sacred Heart. Precious Blood of Jesus, save us! Immaculate Heart of Mary, pray for us! Sacred Heart of Jesus, have mercy on us! Amen.

O Jesus, through the immaculate heart of Mary, I offer you my prayers, works, joys, and sufferings of this day in union with the holy sacrifice of the Mass throughout the world. I offer them for all the intentions of your Sacred Heart: the salvation of souls, reparation for sin, the reunion of all Christians. I offer them for the intentions of our bishops and of all the apostles of prayer, and in particular for those recommended by our Holy Father this month. Amen.

THE DIVINE PRAISES

The Divine Praises are recited at the end of Benediction of the Blessed Sacrament, a devotion consisting of hymns and prayers before the Eucharist exposed on the altar in a monstrance. The priest says each phrase, and the congregation repeats it. Following the Divine Praises, the Eucharist is returned to the tabernacle. You can also recite the Divine Praises privately or with others outside of Benediction. They are a great way to thank and praise God, the Holy Family, and the angels and saints.

V. Blessed be God. R. *Blessed be God.*
V. Blessed be his holy name. R. . . .
V. Blessed be Jesus Christ, true God and true man.
V. Blessed be the name of Jesus.

V. Blessed be his Most Sacred Heart.
V. Blessed be his Most Precious Blood.
V. Blessed be Jesus in the Most Holy Sacrament of the altar.
V. Blessed be the Holy Spirit, the Paraclete.
V. Blessed be the great Mother of God, Mary most holy.
V. Blessed be her holy and Immaculate Conception.
V. Blessed be her glorious Assumption.
V. Blessed be the name of Mary, Virgin and Mother.
V. Blessed be St. Joseph, her most chaste spouse.
V. Blessed be God in his angels and in his saints.

NOVENAS

A novena is a series of prayers said for nine consecutive days, to ask God's help or to thank him. The nine days represent the time that the apostles and the Blessed Virgin Mary spent praying between the ascension of Jesus and Pentecost, when the Holy Spirit would descend on them.

There are many novenas to specific saints, to the Virgin Mary, to the Holy Spirit, and for certain feasts. You can find novenas online, at your parish, and at Catholic bookstores.

LITANIES

A litany is a series of invocations followed by a response. They are prayed in public liturgical services and in private devotions and are intended to implore God's aid and mercy and to praise him. The invocations are usually announced by a cantor, priest, or deacon, and the congregation responds.

A popular litany is the Litany of the Saints, often included in the liturgy of the Easter Vigil, at ordinations, and in other special situations.

THE ROSARY

The word of God is living and effective, sharper than any two-edged sword, penetrating even between soul and spirit.
Hebrews 4:12

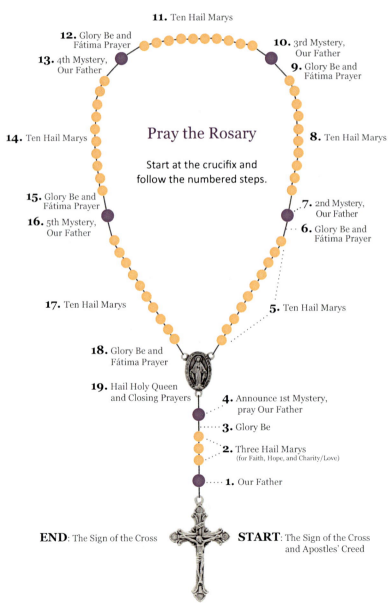

Rosary Schedule

Mondays and Saturdays: Joyful
Tuesdays and Fridays: Sorrowful
Wednesdays: Glorious
Thursdays: Luminous

Sundays:
Advent and Christmas: Joyful
Lent: Sorrowful
Easter and Ordinary: Glorious

Order of Prayers

- Sign of the Cross
- Apostles' Creed, Our Father, Hail Mary (3 times), Glory Be
- For each decade: announce the mystery, read the Scripture passage (optional), Our Father, Hail Mary (10 times), Glory Be, Fátima Prayer
- Closing prayers
- Sign of the Cross

Apostles' Creed

I believe in God, the Father almighty, Creator of heaven and earth, and in Jesus Christ, his only Son, our Lord, who was conceived by the Holy Spirit, born of the Virgin Mary, suffered under Pontius Pilate, was crucified, died and was buried; he descended into hell; on the third day he rose again from the dead; he ascended into heaven, and is seated at the right hand of God the Father almighty; from there he will come to judge the living and the dead.

I believe in the Holy Spirit, the holy catholic Church, the communion of saints, the forgiveness of sins, the resurrection of the body, and life everlasting.

Amen.

Closing Prayers

Hail Holy Queen, Mother of mercy, our life, our sweetness and our hope. To thee do we cry, poor banished children of Eve; to thee do we send up our sighs, mourning and weeping in this valley of tears. Turn then, most gracious Advocate, thine eyes of mercy toward us, and after this our exile, show unto us the blessed fruit of thy womb, Jesus. O clement, O loving, O sweet Virgin Mary!

Pray for us O Holy Mother of God, that we may be made worthy of the promises of Christ.

Let us pray. O God whose only begotten Son by his life, death, and resurrection has purchased for us the rewards of eternal life; grant, we beseech thee, that meditating upon these mysteries of the most holy rosary of the Blessed Virgin Mary, we may imitate what they contain and obtain what they promise through the same Christ our Lord. Amen.

THE JOYFUL MYSTERIES

> **Our Father**
> Our Father, who art in heaven, hallowed be thy name; thy kingdom come; thy will be done on earth as it is in heaven. Give us this day our daily bread; and forgive us our trespasses as we forgive those who trespass against us; and lead us not into temptation, but deliver us from evil. Amen.
>
> **Hail Mary**
> Hail Mary, full of grace, the Lord is with thee; blessed art thou among women, and blessed is the fruit of thy womb, Jesus. Holy Mary, Mother of God, pray for us sinners now and at the hour of our death. Amen.
>
> **Glory Be**
> Glory be to the Father, the Son, and the Holy Spirit; as it was in the beginning, is now, and ever shall be, world without end. Amen.

The Annunciation
Then the angel said to her, "Do not be afraid, Mary, for you have found favor with God. Behold, you will conceive in your womb and bear a son, and you shall name him Jesus." (Luke 1:30-31)

The Visitation
When Elizabeth heard Mary's greeting, the infant leaped in her womb, and Elizabeth, filled with the holy Spirit, cried out in a loud voice and said, "Most blessed are you among women, and blessed is the fruit of your womb. (Luke 1:41-42)

The Birth of Jesus
The angel said to them, "Do not be afraid; for behold, I proclaim to you good news of great joy that will be for all the people. For today in the city of David a savior has been born for you who is Messiah and Lord. (Luke 2:10-11)

The Presentation in the Temple
"Now, Master, you may let your servant go in peace, according to your word, for my eyes have seen your salvation, which you prepared in sight of all the peoples, a light for revelation to the Gentiles, and glory for your people Israel." (Luke 2:29-32)

Finding Jesus in the Temple
After three days they found him in the temple, sitting in the midst of the teachers, listening to them and asking them questions, and all who heard him were astounded at his understanding and his answers. (Luke 2:46-47)

THE SORROWFUL MYSTERIES

The Agony in the Garden
"Father, if you are willing, take this cup away from me; still, not my will but yours be done." And to strengthen him an angel from heaven appeared to him. He was in such agony and he prayed so fervently that his sweat became like drops of blood falling on the ground. (Luke 22:42-44)

The Scourging at the Pillar
Pilate said to them, "Why? What evil has he done?" They only shouted the louder, "Crucify him." So Pilate, wishing to satisfy the crowd, released Barabbas to them and, after he had Jesus scourged, handed him over to be crucified. (Mark 15:14-15)

The Crowning with Thorns
They stripped off his clothes and threw a scarlet military cloak about him. Weaving a crown out of thorns, they placed it on his head, and a reed in his right hand. And kneeling before him, they mocked him, saying, "Hail, King of the Jews!" They spat upon him and took the reed and kept striking him on the head. (Matthew 27 28-30)

The Carrying of the Cross
[A]nd carrying the cross himself he went out to what is called the Place of the Skull, in Hebrew, Golgotha. (John 19:17)

The Crucifixion and Death
After this, aware that everything was now finished, in order that the scripture might be fulfilled, Jesus said, "I thirst." There was a vessel filled with common wine. So they put a sponge soaked in wine on a sprig of hyssop and put it up to his mouth. When Jesus had taken the wine, he said, "It is finished." And bowing his head, he handed over the spirit. (John 19:28-30)

Fátima Prayer
O my Jesus, forgive us of our sins. Save us from the fires of hell. Lead all souls to heaven, especially those in most need of thy mercy.

THE GLORIOUS MYSTERIES

Our Father
Our Father, who art in heaven, hallowed be thy name; thy kingdom come; thy will be done on earth as it is in heaven. Give us this day our daily bread; and forgive us our trespasses as we forgive those who trespass against us; and lead us not into temptation, but deliver us from evil. Amen

Hail Mary
Hail Mary, full of grace, the Lord is with thee; blessed art thou among women, and blessed is the fruit of thy womb, Jesus. Holy Mary, Mother of God, pray for us sinners now and at the hour of our death. Amen.

Glory Be
Glory be to the Father, the Son, and the Holy Spirit; as it was in the beginning, is now, and ever shall be, world without end. Amen.

The Resurrection
They said to them, "Why do you seek the living one among the dead? He is not here, but he has been raised. Remember what he said to you while he was still in Galilee, that the Son of Man must be handed over to sinners and be crucified, and rise on the third day." (Luke 24:5-7)

The Ascension
"You will be my witnesses in Jerusalem, throughout Judea and Samaria, and to the ends of the earth." When he had said this, as they were looking on, he was lifted up, and a cloud took him from their sight. (Acts 1:8-9)

The Descent of the Holy Spirit
And suddenly there came from the sky a noise like a strong driving wind, and it filled the entire house in which they were. Then there appeared to them tongues as of fire, which parted and came to rest on each one of them. And they were all filled with the holy Spirit and began to speak in different tongues, as the Spirit enabled them to proclaim. (Acts 2:2-4)

The Assumption of Mary into Heaven
Arise, my friend, my beautiful one, and come! My dove in the clefts of the rock, in the secret recesses of the cliff, Let me see your face, let me hear your voice, For your voice is sweet, and your face is lovely." (Song of Songs 2:13-14)

Mary is Crowned Queen of Heaven and Earth
A great sign appeared in the sky, a woman clothed with the sun, with the moon under her feet, and on her head a crown of twelve stars. (Revelation 12:1)

THE LUMINOUS MYSTERIES

The Baptism in the Jordan
It happened in those days that Jesus came from Nazareth of Galilee and was baptized in the Jordan by John. On coming up out of the water he saw the heavens being torn open and the Spirit, like a dove, descending upon him. And a voice came from the heavens, "You are my beloved Son; with you I am well pleased." (Mark 1:9-11)

The Wedding Feast at Cana
When the wine ran short, the mother of Jesus said to him, "They have no wine." [And] Jesus said to her, "Woman, how does your concern affect me? My hour has not yet come." His mother said to the servers, "Do whatever he tells you." (John 2:3-5)

The Proclamation of the Kingdom of God
After John had been arrested, Jesus came to Galilee proclaiming the gospel of God: "This is the time of fulfillment. The kingdom of God is at hand. Repent, and believe in the gospel." (Mark 1:14-15)

The Transfiguration
After six days Jesus took Peter, James, and John his brother, and led them up a high mountain by themselves. And he was transfigured before them; his face shone like the sun and his clothes became white as light. And behold, Moses and Elijah appeared to them, conversing with him. (Matthew 17:1-3)

Institution of the Eucharist
Then he took the bread, said the blessing, broke it, and gave it to them, saying, "This is my body, which will be given for you; do this in memory of me." And likewise the cup after they had eaten, saying, "This cup is the new covenant in my blood, which will be shed for you." (Luke 22:19-20)

Fátima Prayer
O my Jesus, forgive us of our sins. Save us from the fires of hell. Lead all souls to heaven, especially those in most need of thy mercy.

THE CHAPLET OF DIVINE MERCY

The Lord revealed himself as the Divine Mercy to St. Faustina Kowalska, a Polish nun, during the 1930s. He gave her this chaplet, which is recited using rosary beads:

Make the sign of the cross with the crucifix: In the name of the Father, and of the Son, and of the Holy Spirit. Amen.

Opening Prayers (on the first bead)

You expired, Jesus, but the source of life gushed forth for souls, and the ocean of mercy opened up for the whole world. O Fount of Life, unfathomable Divine Mercy, envelop the whole world and empty yourself out upon us.

O Blood and Water, which gushed forth from the Heart of Jesus as a fountain of mercy for us, I trust in you! (Repeat three times)

Our Father, Hail Mary, Apostles' Creed (on the next three beads)

Eternal Father, I offer you the Body and Blood, soul and divinity of your dearly beloved Son, Our Lord, Jesus Christ, in atonement for our sins and those of the whole world. (on the large single bead of each decade)

For the sake of his sorrowful passion, have mercy on us and on the whole world. (on the ten small beads of each decade)

Closing Prayers

Holy God, Holy Mighty One, Holy Immortal One, have mercy on us and on the whole world. (Repeat three times)

Eternal God, in whom mercy is endless and the treasury of compassion inexhaustible, look kindly upon us, and increase your mercy in us, that in difficult moments we might not despair nor become despondent, but with great confidence submit ourselves to your holy will, which is Love and Mercy itself.

SUGGESTED READING

- *Catechism of the Catholic Church*, part 4, "Christian Prayer."

- *Prayer Primer: Igniting a Fire Within*, Fr. Thomas Dubay, SM.

13

CATHOLIC CALENDAR

*There is an appointed time for everything,
and a time for every affair under the heavens.*
Ecclesiastes 3:1

ADVENT

The Church year begins with Advent, the season leading up to the celebration of Christmas, the birth of Jesus. Advent is a time to reflect on the wondrous generosity of God and his great love in lowering himself to become man. During this celebration the Church "makes present this ancient expectancy of the Messiah" (*CCC*, 524), as we recall the coming of Jesus as an infant and anticipate his second coming in glory.

The season of Advent begins about four weeks before Christmas and ends Christmas Eve. Catholic churches have Advent

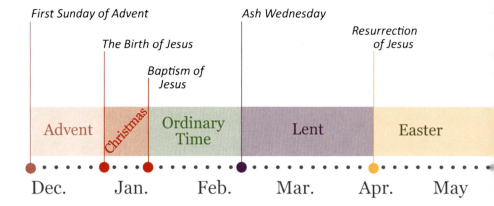

wreaths with candles: one candle is lit the first Sunday, two the second, and so on. Many Catholics have wreaths in their homes. *Magnificat* and other Catholic publications offer prayers and readings to accompany the lighting of the Advent wreath and aid reflection on the meaning of the season.

As we contemplate the unfathomable generosity of God, we also strive to be generous in offering support to those in need. It is wonderful to have family traditions that center on Christ and the importance of his coming. Many parishes have special events during Advent, such as a mission night with an inspiring speaker, a penance service at which all can receive the healing sacrament of reconciliation.

CHRISTMAS

The Christmas season begins with the vigil (late afternoon and evening) Masses on Christmas Eve. We celebrate the coming of Christ to our world and to our hearts. He came to die for our

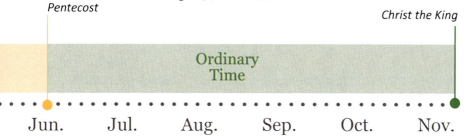

salvation. Where would we be without Christ?

Nativity scenes and Christmas trees are popular both in churches and homes, as reminders of God's great gift to us of new life in Christ. Because God has given to us abundantly, we give gifts during this season to our families, friends, and those in need.

We celebrate the feast of the Holy Family on the first Sunday after Christmas. Jesus, Mary, and Joseph are great examples for the Christian family. We ask for their intercession in becoming the "domestic church" (*CCC*, 2204).

Other feasts during this season include that of St. Stephen, the first Christian martyr; St. John the evangelist; and the Holy Innocents, whom Herod killed in his pursuit of the king of the Jews (see Matthew 2:16-18). The Feast of the Epiphany, celebrated in the United States on the second Sunday after Christmas, recognizes the coming of the Magi to worship "the newborn king of the Jews" (Matthew 2:2). It marks the first revelation of Christ to the nations. "Lord, every nation on earth will adore you" (Psalm 72:11) is the psalm response for this feast.

The Christmas season ends on the third Sunday with the

feast of the Baptism of the Lord. At that time, the Church celebrates when the Father revealed Jesus as "my beloved Son, with whom I am well pleased" (Matthew 3:17).

LENT

Lent is the forty days leading up to Easter. It begins on Ash Wednesday, six and a half weeks before Easter. This is a good day to attend Mass; the ashes we receive on the forehead remind us of our need for repentance and our reliance on God.

During Lent the Church calls us to do things that will bring us closer to Christ—specifically prayer, fasting, and almsgiving. Prayer helps build our relationship with Christ. Additional reading of the Bible, the *Catechism*, and other spiritual books will aid our prayer. Often parishes have an inspiring mission speaker and a penance service, offering the sacrament of reconciliation to all who attend.

Fasting involves self-denial, staying away from worldly things to which we are attached. The Church prescribes abstinence from meat on all Fridays during Lent and on Ash Wednesday, the first day of Lent. We are to fast on Ash Wednesday and Good Friday, the day commemorating Christ's death, in a manner consistent with our physical capability. Lent is also a season for giving time and money to charity.

EASTER

Lent ends with the Easter triduum, which extends from the evening of Holy Thursday to the evening of Easter Sunday.

These three days are liturgically one day, as together they celebrate Christ's paschal mystery.

On Holy Thursday evening, the Mass celebrates the Last Supper, when Christ initiated the Eucharist and the priesthood. Often the pastor washes the feet of twelve members of the congregation, in commemoration of Christ's action and his call to "wash one another's feet" (John 13:14). After Mass there is Eucharistic adoration. We remember Jesus' agony in the Garden of Gethsemane, where he prayed to the Father in anticipation of his passion.

Good Friday is a solemn day for meditating on the passion and death of Jesus. It is a day of fasting and abstinence: Catholics eat no meat and, to the extent their health allows, have only one regular meal and two small meals. Most parishes have a Good Friday liturgy with an opportunity to venerate the cross—to approach the cross and kiss it—and receive Holy Communion, though there is no Mass. Many parishes proceed to the Stations of the Cross, meditations on fourteen moments in Christ's passion and death, represented by images or by actors.

Holy Saturday is a somber day recalling Christ's stay in the tomb and his liberation of the dead.

Easter, the most important celebration of the Church year, begins with the Vigil Mass, on Holy Saturday evening. The Vigil Mass can run for two to four hours, with the proclamation of several Scripture readings from both the Old and New Testaments. This Mass often includes baptism, first Communion, and confirmation for people coming into the Catholic Church. (This is an example of a time when the bishop allows the priest to administer confirmation.) The Mass is a joyful and grace-filled experience. Easter Sunday Masses the following morning continue the celebration of gratitude and joy.

ORDINARY TIME

Tempus per annum, meaning "time through the year," is popularly known as Ordinary Time. *Ordinary* here refers not to ho-hum routine but to the way the weeks are ordered or numbered, from one to thirty-four. Ordinary Time starts after the feast of the Baptism of the Lord in January, extends to the Tuesday before Ash Wednesday in the spring, picks up again after Pentecost, and ends the day before Advent begins.

Ordinary Time is a season to reflect on the entirety of Christ's life and his victory over sin and death. It is a time for spiritual growth: deepening our relationship with Christ and striving to put him first in our lives. The priests' vestments are a vibrant green color, signifying this growth and hope. Ordinary Time can actually be something quite extraordinary if we stay focused on God as the center of life. The last Sunday of Ordinary Time is the solemnity of Christ the King. Then the following Sunday is the first Sunday of Advent, and the whole liturgical year begins anew.

HOLY DAYS OF OBLIGATION

God's third commandment is to keep holy the Lord's day by attending Mass and refraining from work. In addition to Sundays, the Church has discerned certain holy days as being very important, and she calls us to attend Mass on those days as well. We should look at these obligations as opportunities to adjust our priorities if necessary and to make sure God is at the center of our lives. Below is the list of the holy days of obligation for the United States. For other countries, please check online.

- January 1, the solemnity of Mary, Mother of God

- Thursday of the Sixth Week of Easter, the solemnity of the Ascension (celebrated in some dioceses on the following Sunday)

- August 15, the solemnity of the Assumption of the Blessed Virgin Mary

- November 1, the solemnity of All Saints

- December 8, the solemnity of the Immaculate Conception

- December 25, the solemnity of the Nativity of Our Lord Jesus Christ

SOLEMNITIES, FEASTS, AND MEMORIALS

The Church designates certain days as solemnities, feasts, or memorials.

Solemnities are the highest celebrations on the Catholic calendar, such as Easter, Christmas, Pentecost, and the holy days of obligation. The Mass on these days always includes the Gloria and the Creed.

Feasts are celebrations of certain saints, including the archangels and most of the apostles. The Gloria is included in the Mass on these special days.

Memorials celebrate the remaining saints. Some memorials must be observed in the liturgy, while others are optional. The Gloria is not included in the Mass on these days.

It is a great practice to follow the liturgical calendar and celebrate important holy days throughout the year. You can synchronize the Catholic calendar to your own Google calendar by visiting this link: http://universalis.com/calendar.htm. Attending Mass and saying a novena leading up to the holy day are edifying ways to celebrate solemnities, feasts, and memorials.

MONTHLY DEVOTIONS

Catholic custom sanctifies each month of the year with one or more devotions:

- **January**: The Holy Name of Jesus

- **February**: The Sacred Passion and the Holy Family

- **March**: St. Joseph

- **April**: The Holy Eucharist

- **May**: The Blessed Virgin Mary

- **June**: The Sacred Heart of Jesus

- **July**: The Precious Blood of Jesus

- **August**: The Immaculate Heart of Mary

- **September**: The Seven Sorrows of Mary

- **October**: The Holy Rosary

- **November**: The Holy Souls in Purgatory

- **December**: The Divine Infancy and the Immaculate Conception

SUGGESTED READING

- *Behold, He Comes: Meditations on the Incarnation* and *The King, Crucified and Risen: Meditations on the Passion and Glory of Christ,* FR. Benedict Groeschel, CFR.

- *Catholic and Loving It: Traditions for a New Generation,* Sabitha Narendran and Andrew Salzmann.

- *Feast! Real Food, Reflections, and Simple Living for the Christian Year*, Daniel and Haley Stewart.

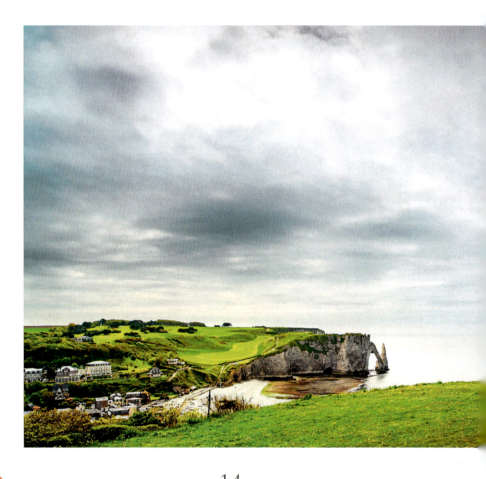

14
GROWING IN THE CATHOLIC FAITH

Everyone who listens to these words of mine and acts on them will be like a wise man who built his house on rock.

Matthew 7:24

BUILDING A CATHOLIC FAITH FOUNDATION

It is important to build a strong foundation in the Catholic faith. First, it will provide clarity and security in your walk with God. Jesus wants a personal bond with you that grows each day. Understanding the teachings of the Church he started is a big part of knowing him.

Second, a strong Catholic foundation will also equip you to share the faith with others, as Jesus calls us to do (see Mark 16:15).

You will be able to embrace, live out, and proclaim the objective truth that the Church proclaims.

I sincerely hope that God has spoken to you through this book and ignited a desire inside of you to grow closer to him. The combination of encountering Jesus Christ and seeing how he is present to us in his Church, the Catholic Church, is a miracle. I believe that the more we understand this miracle, the better the world will be. I encourage you to take action steps to align your life with God and start, or continue, your faith journey.

And faith is a journey. The process of growing in virtue, becoming more like Jesus Christ, will not end until we complete this earthly pilgrimage.

I hope this book will be a good reference for you and for family and friends who have questions about the faith. I've only scratched the surface of Catholic teaching; the books recommended with each topic offer much more information and inspiration. I suggest you prayerfully pick a few items from "A Lively Catholic's To-Do List" in chapter 10 to help you grow in your faith. Most importantly, stay close to God through prayer, Scripture reading, and the sacraments.

> May the God of hope fill you with all joy and peace in believing, so that you may abound in hope by the power of the holy Spirit. (Romans 15:13)

Here are some additional resources to assist you on your faith journey:

EWTN, THE ETERNAL WORD TELEVISION NETWORK

I have found this global Catholic television (and radio!) network to be phenomenal. Most of its programs are live-streamed on Facebook and YouTube. You can also download a free app onto your smartphone or tablet, so you can watch and listen from anywhere. The EWTN website, ewtn.com, gives the program schedule and provides a host of other resources for Catholic life.

Here are some of my favorite programs from EWTN:

• For news and discussion of important Catholic issues, including the pro-life movement, religious freedom, and more, *Catholic Connection* with Teresa Tomeo and *Kresta in the Afternoon* with Al Kresta are both on EWTN radio every day.

• For Catholic teachings and apologetics, Dr. David Anders presents the live call-in show *Called to Communion* on both radio and television. On *Catholic Answers Live*, apologists and scholars welcome questions from Catholics, atheists, and people of other beliefs.

• For questions on mental health and family issues, Dr. Greg and Lisa Popcak respond to live calls on *More 2 Life*.

• For everyday Catholic guidance, tune in to Johnnette Benkovic Williams's *Women of Grace*, on both radio and television; *Take 2*, with Jerry Usher and Debbie Georgianni, on radio; and *Open Line*, hosted by several apologists.

• For growing closer to God, Fr. John Riccardo's recorded teachings are featured on *Christ Is the Answer*.

• Marcus Grodi presents inspiring conversion stories on *The Journey Home*, on both radio and TV.

DOCUMENTARIES

• *Convinced* presents stories of conversion to Catholicism, including those of a former abortionist, several former atheists, Protestant pastors, and more (Don Johnson Evangelistic Ministries, donjohnsonministries.org).

• *Fearless* offers amazing evidence of the power of the Holy Spirit, especially in evangelism and healing (Rooster Power Productions, fearlessdocumentary.net).

• *City of Saints* is a seven-part film series with true stories of God's action in individuals' lives (St. Michael's Abbey, cityofsaints.com).

CATHOLIC NEWS

• *Crisis Magazine*, "A Voice for the Faithful Catholic Laity," emails daily articles on current Catholic issues (crisismagazine.com).

• *National Catholic Register*, paper and online, offers Catholics news (ncregister.com). Also see Catholic News Agency online (catholicnewsagency.com).

OTHER RESOURCES

• From Fr. Larry Richards comes thereasonforourhope.org: homilies, books, and more.

- Claritas U is an online Catholic community that wants to help you "get clear about your faith" (Claritasu.com).

- Avila Institute offers online courses in spiritual formation and daily inspirational emails (avilainstitute.com).

Retreats

Many dioceses and parishes offer retreats. ACTS is a parish-based, three-day event that fosters an experience of Christ's love, leading to commitment to him and his mission (Actsmissions.org).

Conferences

- Fullness of Truth, based in Texas, offers Catholic family and evangelization conferences throughout the country (fullnessoftruth.org).

- Pilgrimage Center of Hope, in San Antonio, Texas, sponsors pilgrimages to the Holy Land, Rome, Guadalupe, and other places of Catholic interest, as well as conferences (pilgrimcenterofhope.org).

- The Franciscan University of Steubenville in Ohio offers summer conferences for youth, priests, budding evangelists, catechists, and more (steubenvilleconferences.com).

- FOCUS, the Fellowship of Catholic University Students, offers an annual SEEK conference for university students (focus.org).

- Called & Gifted Discernment Process includes the Called & Gifted workshop, a spiritual gifts interview, and teaching on discerning and developing your gifts (Catherine of Siena Institute, siena.org).

NOTES

1. C.S. Lewis, *The Problem of Pain*, New York: HarperCollins, 1996, p. 92.

2. Vic Scaravilli, "Catholic Basics," YouTube video, 69 video segments, 2008, https://youtu.be/17SXYlZvEbU. Also available at http://www.catholicdigitalstudio.com/.

3. *Baltimore Catechism* #3, 1891 version, http://www.baltimore-catechism.com/index.htm, Q. 150 (emphasis added).

4. St. Ignatius of Antioch, "Epistle to the Smyrneans", Ch. 8.

5. D.D. Emmons, "Did the Council of Trent Change the Church?," Our Sunday Visitor, May 29, 012, https://www.osv.com/Article/TabId/493/ArtMID/13569/ArticleID/2565/Did-the-Council-of-Trent-Change-the-Church.aspx.

6. "The List of Popes," The Catholic Encyclopedia Vol. 12., (New York: Robert Appleton Company, 1911), accessed April 26, 2018, http://www.newadvent.org/cathen/12272b.htm.

7. Father Larry Richards, *The Mass Explained*, (Lighthouse Catholic Media 2009), Audio CD. Also available on YouTube: https://youtu.be/PPvx2IPsOxY.

8. Ibid.

9. Ibid.

10. Ibid.

11. See Neal Lozano, *Unbound: A Practical Guide to Deliverance.* (Baker Publishing, 2010).

12. Pope John Paul II, "Evangelium Vitae" ["The Gospel of Life"], 28.

13. Pope Paul VI, "Humanae Vitae" ["Of Human Life"], 11-12.

14. Ibid., 17.

15. John Hardon, *The Catholic Dictionary* (Crown Publishing Group, 2013), p. 159.

16. Pope St. John Paul II, "Ecclesia de Eucharistia" ["On the Eucharist and the Church"], 25.

17. "Significance of the Sign of the Cross - Bert Ghezzi on the Meaning Behind the Ancient Gesture," ZENIT International News Agency, 2004, accessed at Eternal Word Television Network, https://www.ewtn.com/library/liturgy/zsigncro.htm. Further study on the sign of the cross can be done by reading Bert Ghezzi's book, *The Sign of the Cross: Recovering the Power of the Ancient Prayer* (Loyola Press, 2006).

18. Ibid.

Made in United States
North Haven, CT
21 April 2024